FRED'S MEMOIRS

I0346699

By
Raymond Frederick Blount

FRED'S MEMOIRS

Author: Raymond Frederick Blount

Copyright © Raymond Frederick Blount (2026)

The right of Raymond Frederick Blount to be identified as author of this work has been asserted by the author in accordance with section 77 and 78 of the Copyright, Designs and Patents Act 1988.

First Published in 2026

ISBN 978-1-83538-932-4 (Paperback)
978-1-83538-933-1 (E-Book)

Cover Design and Book Layout by:
Maple Publishers
www.maplepublishers.com

Published by:
Maple Publishers
Fairbourne Drive, Atterbury,
Milton Keynes,
MK10 9RG, UK
www.maplepublishers.com

The views expressed in this work are solely those of the author and do not reflect the opinions of Publishers, and the Publisher hereby disclaims any responsibility for them. This book should not be used as a substitute for the advice of a competent authority, admitted or authorized to advise on the subjects covered.

A CIP catalogue record for this title is available from the British Library.

All rights reserved. No part of this book may be reproduced or translated by any form or by any means, electronic or mechanical, including photocopying, recording or by any information storage and retrieval system without written permission from the author.

Fred Blount

To wish you a very happy

90th Birthday

John & Nancy Jefferis

12th February 2005

Fred handwrote his memoires, recording stories from his life and work in his own words. His good friend, John kindly typed them up and presented Fred with the finished collection – together with a floppy disk – on his 90th birthday. Now as Fred's business proudly celebrates its 80th year, the family has chosen to print his memoirs as a lasting tribute to him and the life he built.

Fred Blount died on

29th December 2007 aged 92 years

Work Carried Out by R.F. Blount,
Plumbing & Heating Engineers,
Northfield Avenue, Kettering
at The Kettering Parish Church of SS Peter & Paul

In the 1950s and during the early days of Frank Pearce's time as Rector at St Peter & Paul, the Churchwardens were Frank Valentine and Walter Pringle, and at this time some leakage was being experienced in the roof of the North Aisle. I was asked by Frank Valentine if I would carry out an inspection, to ascertain the extent of any repairs that may be necessary. This turned out to be the commencement of an interesting programme of events and repair work.

We duly visited the Church with ladders, and with my first steps on to the roof I knew, without any further inspection, that the problem was serious, and proceeded very gingerly to the middle of the roof to the position of the drips where the top sheets overlapped the bottom sheets and carefully lifted the sheets of lead to expose the timbers beneath. I reached out to the remains of boards, which fell away in dust; the rafters also fell away in dust.

Before I replaced the lead to make it watertight, I fetched Jack Newman, the Verger at that time, to witness the damage and then replaced the lead temporarily and duly reported to the Rector and Churchwardens.

It was decided very quickly to get immediate estimates for replacing all boarding and timbers and for removing, re-casting, and re-laying all lead work.

The outcome of this was that, Messrs Tailby & Son of Desborough were employed to replace all the timbers, and we organised and carried out the re-casting and re-laying of the 7 lb cast lead.

But before all this happened, there was an interesting observation I made regarding the underfelt previously used which was inodorous hairfelt, which was the accepted under-felt used for this work. It is about ½ inch thick and very similar to carpet underfelt.

Mr Scott was the architect employed at this time as Church Architect and I pointed out to him that when we removed the old lead, the underfelt was soaking wet, all but about the bottom 5 or 6 ft due to the fact that under the right circumstances condensation was forming on the underside of the lead sheet, which was soaked up by the felt and the fact also that the sun never reached this part of the roof, because of the wall and windows of the Main Nave, except the last 5 or 6 ft, perhaps more during the summer months.

We discarded the inodorous felt and used Class C building paper under the new lead. Class C building paper is heavy-duty brown paper; 2 sheets stuck together with tar – a brown-paper tar sandwich.

This was obviously the answer to a North-facing lead-covered roof in this particular site and situation. But as we subsequently found out, it did not solve all problems of roofs in differing aspects, North, South, East or West.

About this time, a restoration drive of the Church fabric was commenced, and also about this time I was asked by the Rector, Frank Pearce, to be the Rector's Warden, which after some careful thought and consideration, I accepted. This was meant to be for 3 years, but I actually spent a term of 10 years, with Ken Bacon, 1975 to 1985 as Rector's Warden.

The next major repair was the stripping, re-casting and re-laying of the lead on the South Aisle. We duly estimated for this work, and were appointed to this work which was carried out with no problems, other than the plumber who was carrying out this work, went sick for several months with Housemaid's Knee. By this time, owing to the pressure of work and the amount of work that we were getting, I was occupied full-time in the office, but I had in the past experienced the painful effects of Housemaid's Knee. The outcome of this was that I had to get my overalls on and complete the work myself. We used Class C building paper as underfelt on the South Aisle, which was satisfactory. The problem with all lead roofs facing South is the heat from the sun, and expansion of the lead. This is overcome by regulating the size of the cast lead sheets to a maximum size of 24 sq. ft. or less.

The next part of the restoration programme was the Nave. Again, we estimated and tendered for this, but this time we lost the work, and Anglian Lead of Norwich carried out this work.

But a strange thing happened shortly after the work was completed. It was either Easter Sunday or Whitsunday; it was a very hot, sunny day, and everyone in the Church was amazed to see puddles on the floor all the length of the Middle Aisle, and it had not rained for several days.

Anglian Lead had used Class C building paper as an underfelt, just as we would have done, and had already done on the North and South Aisles.

I looked at the main ridge beams in the apex of the roof, and could see that it was soaking wet.

Immediately, after the Service, the Rector came to me and said 'What is this?' to which I replied 'Condensation and if we do not do something quickly, the roof timbers will go rotten.' Then came the inevitable question: 'Why does this happen now - it has never happened before?'

The answer to this was, that the underfelt had been changed from inodorous felt to Class C building paper. Before, the heat and wet air was obviously getting through the hair felt, breathing in a manner of speaking. There may have been some condensation on the underside of the lead, but the felt would have soaked this up and got rid of it by evaporation.

However, we had to find a quick cure for the situation.

In the past, I had developed a correspondence association with the Lead Development Association who, as the name implies, were promoting the use of lead. I used to receive free publications on all the new developments, and a monthly newssheet on work currently in progress.

I wrote to them, and they immediately sent a man to see the problem. He made a number of alternative suggestions, mostly involving cutting large holes in the structure, and fitting extract fans.

I was not very keen on any of these suggestions, as the cutting of holes in walls etc., would not be received very kindly. However, a few weeks after this, I received the periodical newssheet from the Lead Development Association and an article in this paper caught my eye. It dealt with the same problem that we had, where a new church in the London area where in two years from being built, the roof timbers had gone rotten and a whole new roof had been constructed. It was a large pyramid modern-design roof. They, like us, had used Class C building paper with exactly the same problem, and result.

In the new roof, they had constructed a series of lead vent pipes near the apex of the roof, by cutting holes through the lead and roof boards, and lead-burning 1" diameter lead pipes on to the roofing sheets, protruding about 4" into the church, and extending vertically about 12", with a return bend on the top, discharging the condensate on to the roof.

I showed the article to the Rector, who asked us to carry out this work. We immediately carried out this work, by lead-burning a series of vents on alternate sides of the ridge at about 15 ft intervals. This proved successful and no further condensation has been seen. We did not involve Anglian Lead in this work, because they had done a first-class job.

The introduction of Class C building paper was a new material at that time, and with it came condensation problems, but there is an answer to all problems.

When building paper is used in a situation where a ridge roof traps air, ventilation must by some means be introduced to prevent the accumulation of wet air, which is also aggravated by hot- or warm-air heating. So, the fact that Kettering Parish Church of St Peter & Paul has still got a sound timber roof, is our claim to fame.

Other Church Work

About this time, we were doing a great deal of cast lead work in the county. One of these contracts was at Litchborough Church, where we removed, re-cast and re-laid the South Aisle and one of the old sheets had a date on it, about 1745, well over 200 years old.

Another small job that we were asked to estimate was the top of the tower of St Giles Church, Northampton. We were successful and carried out this work, but, when I was estimating this work, I was climbing a long ladder from the belfry floor to a trap door, that opened on to the roof. Near the bottom of the ladder, I noticed some woodworm in the rungs of the ladder, so I was carefully inspecting the rungs. I had nearly got to the trap door, when BONG, the clock struck eleven. I froze on the ladder, until the chime had finished.

The top of the tower was about 30 ft square; as I have already said, a small job, but quite interesting. While we were there, we were asked to inspect the rest of the roof, and report and repair other leaks; this proved very interesting. It was the worst piece of lead work that I had seen anywhere in all my experience. The sheets in many places had been cut short, some of the rolls only ¼" upstand to rolls, where they should have been 3 ½" terminating over the top of the rolls. Many of the rolls were covered with capping pieces over the tops of the rolls, using much more lead, than if the sheets had been initially the right size. You might say, it was a complete waste of good material. I think that, it has since been stripped and re-covered.

Another church that we did quite a bit of work on was Harrington Church, which is situated about ¼ mile outside the village. It was regularly visited by lead thieves and we, for a time, were employed to replace the missing lead. The last repair that we carried out was in the month of November and approximately one month later, before we had sent the bill for our work, over the Christmas Holiday, it was stolen again. After this, some sort of plastic covering was used, a sad conclusion, but under the circumstances, a necessary step.

When it was decided to use a plastic cover, we were asked to put a temporary roofing felt cover on the uncovered part, and the next day we were instructed to remove the remaining lead, ready for the plastic. We spent a whole day removing the lead, and carting it away for crediting and no-one came to ask what we were doing; it is that easy.

The other funny experience on a church I had, was about 1950, when Messrs. George Knight of Meadow Rd/Cromwell Rd, Kettering were instructed to renew the roof timbers on the Saxon Tower at Brigstock, on the side of the main Bell Tower, which terminated just below the Belfry. We were employed to remove the cast lead, which we carefully folded up and stored in the Belfry. Knights completed their work, and we were busy taking the lead from the Belfry and carefully unfolding the lead and re-laying. There was no money for new lead. It was very old cast lead, and we had to replace it in its original state with great care, and with a little lead burning, to one or two holes.

We were dressing out the old lead, concentrating on the work in hand, and suddenly a voice of authority behind me said, 'What do you think you are doing?' Turning round quickly, there was the village constable, head and shoulders through the Belfry window, and without hesitation I said, 'You're too late, mate, we are just putting it back!' I have related this story many times since, and had many a good laugh from it.

Titchmarsh Church was struck by lightning, striking one of the pinnacles on one corner of the tower, toppling the masonry on to the cast lead roof of the tower, also damaging the timber beneath it. The stonework was repaired by a local stonemason, and the boarding was repaired by the local builder who was also Churchwarden at the time. I went over to inspect the damage, in preparation for repair. Fortunately, the Churchwarden was following me up the ladder. I opened the trapdoor to the Belfry, and put my hand on a piece of wood, which to me looked like handrail, but behind me came a sharp warning, 'Don't touch that, it is propping a bell up' and sure enough, when I eventually hauled myself up into the Belfry, I could see it was propping up a large bell. Apparently, they were in the habit of ringing up the bells after they were last used, ready for a flying start next time of use; it would have taken my head off, but for the timely warning from Harold Turner, Churchwarden at that time. The repairs were eventually completed by us.

During my 10 years' time as Churchwarden, which finally finished on my 70th birthday, which also coincided with my retirement from business, we were to be visited by Bishop Feaver for the Confirmation Service. Just as I was about to leave home, the phone rang, and one of the Northamptonshire County Council properties was in trouble with their heating, and being a cold winter's night, was asking for our services.

Panic, what was I going to do? I always put this work first, because first of all were the Old Peoples' Homes, Old Peoples' Hospitals, Police Station, Fire Station, Schools, etc. all over the County.

I started ringing up our various engineers and finally got one to take the call out, but by the time I reached the Church at about a quarter to eight, the Service had been underway for a quarter of an hour. I found John Jefferis, the Deputy Churchwarden standing in for me. We quickly changed places.

After the Service the Bishop said the closing prayers in the Vestry and immediately said 'A miracle has occurred during this Service. I notice the Churchwarden has aged 20 years.' I subsequently found out, that John is just 20 years younger than I am. Bishop Feaver did not miss much. I liked him very much.

The heating of churches was generally introduced at the turn of the century, and in many instances, aggravated the condensation problems to the damage to roof timbers in varying degrees, depending on the structure of the roofs and how much heat was introduced, and directly related to how much, if any, ventilation was existing. Also, depending on what roof covering and underfelt was used.

Before 1900, some warm air systems were used in the simple form of floor warm-air ducts, including cast iron floor grilles, with sometimes, a solid fuel furnace outside the church and sometimes, a solid fuel furnace inside the church in a large chamber under the floor, with steps down for stoking.

Also, from 1700 to 1800, Tortoise Stoves were used, small ones to very large cast-iron ones in some of our large churches and cathedrals.

In the last 50 to 60 years, the radiator or wet systems, fan convectors became popular, partly because of their high outputs, but more importantly, the fans moved the air around, preventing stagnant wet air accumulating in roof areas. I remember in my younger days as a server at St Mary's Church, sitting as was the habit, with my back to the West Wall of the Chancel during the sermon, getting a strong draught down my neck from convection currents, and a draught from the Nave and down the Chancel walls. Most of the heating was in the form of 4" cast-iron pipes and large cast-iron radiators in the Nave. With the introduction of oil-fired, and later gas-fired heating, the problems of condensation increased.

Fred Blount

April 2000

Fred Blount Memoirs 1

Repairs to and Updating of the Heating System of **Kettering Parish Church of SS Peter & Paul and a Brief History of the Heating of Churches**

Probably the first types of church heating systems were in the form of cast iron space heating, solid fuel stoves, similar to Tortoise Stoves, from small simple things with firebrick lining to combustion chamber, and heavy cast iron outer casing to radiate heat. Some of the larger churches and cathedrals had similar appliances, but much larger and more ornate, and complicated with all sorts of complicated radiants, incorporated in the outer casing to give off heat.

Also, about this time many churches had installed a simple form of warm air system, sometimes having an external furnace with a system of under-floor warm air ducts radiating from the furnace, under the floor of the church, with ornate cast iron floor gratings over the ducts. With some of these, I have seen a furnace with steps down into a pit or chamber, inside the church and a chimney in the nearest wall. These systems were used, some of them quite effective, but with all the problems of solid fuel: disposal of ashes, carrying of fuel, etc.

And then came the various forms of water conducted heating systems, around 1800 onwards and including steam heating and high-pressure water systems. The last two mentioned, did not survive long, both being dangerous because surface temperatures were too high and uncontrollable. The insurance companies eventually closed these systems down, as they refused to insure the buildings with steam or high-pressure hot water in them. Both of these systems, or a modern form of these systems are both still used in industry for high-temperature, hot water processes, for instance, where temperatures above boiling point are required.

But particularly, the old high-pressure hot water system was very dangerous, because it consisted of a single endless loop of a $\frac{7}{8}$-inch bore pipe, with a wall thickness of $\frac{1}{4}$ inch, taken round a building with batteries of coils as radiators, and eventually a battery coil inside a brick furnace, and reconnected to the loop. A fire was lit in the boiler chamber, which quickly generated very high temperatures and pressures; a safety valve was fitted in at something like 600 lb/sq., with a surface temperature of something between 500 ºF and 600 ºF. These systems were constructed with only one type of straight connector or socket, with right- and left-hand fine threads. The bends were formed with the use of a forge. The tube ends were accurately machined, one end flat and the other V-shaped.

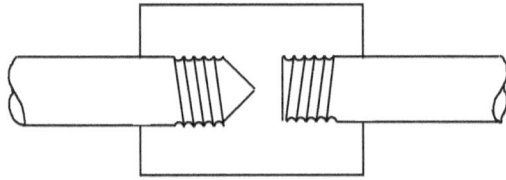

The two ends were drawn together by the right- and left-hand socket with a large Stillson pipe wrench, until a metal-to-metal joint was obtained.

The temperatures obtained were so high, that if they were to touch timber, it ignited and terrible fires and destruction ensued. Also, if anyone accidentally touched or fell on the pipe coils, terrible injuries were inflicted and so insurance of these systems was impossible.

History of Heating Systems at Kettering Parish Church of SS Peter & Paul

The foregoing description of the old high-pressure heating system, I have described in detail, because there was evidence that one of these systems was installed in the church, probably the first heating system, probably in the mid-1800s. In the vestry, I found the remains of one of these systems, a length of high-pressure pipework and a socket, which had probably been left, to avoid damaging the woodwork. But as far as I was able to ascertain, all other traces of the system had been removed.

Next came the low-pressure heating system, approximately 1892, before the common use of pumps. That is why the 3-inch flow pipe from the boiler situated in the boiler house, where the present gas-fired boiler is now, rises to the belfry floor, and is terminated with a 3-inch tee, and descends in 2¾-inch pipe down to low level. This was done to induce circulating pressure, by the extra weight of water in the two descending columns, above the weight in one ascending column. This was installed by J.L. Bacon & Co, Heating & Ventilating Engineers, Dorset Square, London.

We have recently removed this pipework along with other work updating the system, and had difficulty because 2¾-inch pipe and fittings have not been made, since before I started work in 1929, and we had to weld to overcome this problem.

The old system was fed from a tank in the belfry, and had to be fed by town pressure in the vestry periodically, by hosepipe on to a drain cock. This problem was also dealt with, in the recent update of the system.

However, nothing is perfect in this world and although, we have done all that it is possible to do, including actually reducing the head pressure of the system and by so doing, relieving the ageing condition of the very old pipes, radiators and finned tubes in the floor, I am sure that Brian Chapman [the Verger] is also pleased that he no longer has the unpleasant job of backfilling the old system, it did tell us when we had a leak somewhere, which was duly found and repaired, whereas, now the water level is automatically replaced, so someone should keep an eye on the pressure vessel in the boiler room, to see if too much replacement water is being injected.

This brings us up to the time, when the old solid-fuel boiler was converted to oil-firing in 1960 approximately. This served until 1990 approximately, after Suez, after which the cost of oil went up, and then we installed a new gas-fired boiler and gas supply. Next, we had to take up part of the paving outside the West Door, expose the flow and return pipework, replace some badly rusted pipework, test and replace paving.

Which brings us up to the removal of pipework in the tower, as part of preparation to fitting new entrance doors to the West Front and at the same time, introduce a pressurised system, and town pressure, automatic water replacement system. Alright, we have done all we can to bring things up to date, but most of the still existing pipework is over 100 years old, and sometime in the not-too-distant future, a new system of pipework will have to be installed. This is a real situation, and should be carefully kept in mind, and funds built up ready for this situation. It could cost a substantial amount.

The other vitally important item to keep in mind, is the ventilation of the chancel roof, and the importance that all future people responsible for the fabric of the church, are aware of the existence of these vents, and why they are so important. They are not very obvious, unless one actually gets on to the roof, and even then, the importance of them could possibly not be realised, but as I have pointed out earlier, if for any reason, they were removed or blocked off, the timbers of the chancel, even though they are very substantial, would be rotten within two years, and a new timber roof would cost more than a new heating system.

The other modern form of heating used in some churches, is electrical radiant heating or tubular radiant heaters. All forms have their advantages and disadvantages. Electrical radiant heating is almost instantaneous and concentrated in areas where it is wanted, and the same can be said regarding tubular heaters, but against this is the high cost of any form of electrical space heating, and the other disadvantage is the condensation problem. The effect of sudden bursts of heating meeting extreme cold air of churches, is the worst example of condensation problems and so is not the best of choices.

Fred Blount

April 2000

Fred Blount Memoirs 2

R.F. Blount
My Work as a Plumber and Heating Engineer – Part 1

I was educated at Kettering Stamford Road Elementary School, starting at the age of 4 years, Easter 1919. The only thing I remember clearly of this time, is of a girl pulling me out of my chair and dragging me by my feet over the wooden block floor, from which I collected a splinter 2 inches long in my bottom.

My mother took me to the doctor (Dr Roughton, of the Parish Church front gates); he was an old man, with very bad eyesight, wearing glasses that looked like glass pebbles, and after searching and poking about for several painful minutes gave up the search, apologised, saying he could not find the splinter and that it would work its way out. He was right; it came out when my mother was bathing me about 4 or 5 months later. No doubt she was looking for it, but more of that much later.

I progressed through the infant school and moved on to the junior and senior Schools. At this time, I was attending St Mary's Church. I had 6 maiden aunts who took me to church, where I eventually joined the choir at the age of 7, and stayed there until my voice broke, when I became a server.

When I joined at the age of 7, Sid Loasby was Choirmaster and Organist. We had an annual choir outing, when Sid used to take his car, a two-seater with a 'Dicky Boot'; one of the boys sat next to Sid, and two others in the boot with the lid up. This went on for some years until about 1927, when Sid left to become Organist and Choirmaster at St Peter & St Paul.

We had some very good teachers at Stamford Road School. Mr House was Headmaster, Mr Mole 1st assistant, Mr Capp Music Teacher, Mr Lilley, Mr Brown, Miss Middleton and Miss Barnwell. I took and passed my 11 plus, which automatically gave me access to the Central School (now St Andrew's School), but all this time I was having health problems, and my parents decided to keep me at Stamford Road School. (I have never regretted this decision; it worked out for the best).

When I was about 12/13, Mr Capp picked me out from the whole school to sing 'Jerusalem' on Empire Day, when the Mayor and Town Councillors were invited to the celebrations. I don't think I performed at my best - I was too scared. Thinking about this, it would not have been the mayor, because at that time we did not have borough status; he or she would have been head of the Urban District Council.

Eventually, I left school at the age of 14. My father took me down to the Employment Office in Dryland Street; at that time, it was a wooden temporary building. My parents had decided that I was not going into a factory; I was still having health problems. I fancied being a carpenter or electrician, but nothing was available in these directions, so my father enlisted me as a plumber's mate.

My father worked at Freeman Hardy & Willis in the shoe trade.

When we left the employment office, I turned to my father and said 'What is a plumber, Dad?' Well, it was a good choice; I have now been finding out what a plumber is for 71 years, and have enjoyed every minute of it. [A plumber is a worker of and in lead, from the Latin for lead 'plumbum'. There are not many true-to-name plumbers left now].

At Easter 1929, I started working as a plumber's mate on the following Monday morning for W. Burton & Son, Plumbers & Heating Engineers. They had recently moved from the top of West Street, where they had a fire and the premises were burnt out, and moved to Montagu Street; this would have been about 1926, since when Billy Burton, the boss, had retired and moved down to Eastbourne. I used to see him once a year, when he came home for Christmas. I had the job of casting some lead weights for sea fishing on these occasions for him.

I started work for 10 shillings per week; the first Christmas I had half a guinea in my packet, in lieu of a Christmas present. When I showed it to my mother, she explained that it was worth fifteen shillings. To me, it looked like a bright new 1 farthing, which at that time was still legal tender. The milliners' shops would display dress materials and curtains, etc. at one and eleven pence, 3 farthings per yard and similar figures: 1 farthing short of 2 shillings, just the same as they do today, except now it is in pence.

In 1932, we worked on the new Drill Hall; the building contractors were Smith & Bunning in Regent Street, Kettering. This has recently been pulled down, which is a great pity, as it was one of the best-built premises in Kettering.

When I was 19 years of age, J.T. Capps, Plumbing and Heating, borrowed me from Burton's to work for him, while he was on his honeymoon. At that time, there were whispers that W. Burton & Sons were closing down. The son-in-law who was running our side of the business was in poor health, and was going to retire and at the same time young Billy Burton, our boss's son, had for some years been building up quite a good business selling paint, wallpaper, hardware and glass under the heading of Montagu Wallpaper & Paint Co, and he was needing more room and looking to take over our premises. So, I stayed with Tommy Capps until 1945, when I started my own business.

At the time when I moved to J.T. Capps in 1934, when I was 19 years of age, I was beginning to get interested in the work, and was looking round for means of getting to know more about the work. I soon found out, that there were no technical training centres anywhere in reach of Kettering. There were, in fact, no training facilities anywhere in Northamptonshire, the nearest technical schools were in Leicester and Nottingham.

I eventually overcame this setback by doing a 4-year International Correspondence School Course, which incidentally took 6 years to complete: very hard work, very detailed and very thorough, the finest thing that could have happened to me at that time, because at the same time that I was working on the theory of our work, I was engaged in the practical application of the work for 5½ days per week.

One subject at a time was sent to me to work on, starting with Arithmetic, followed by Shop Mensuration, Drawing, Drawing as applied to Plumbing and so on, and one at a time these subjects were studied, and a series of questions were answered at the end of each subject and sent off in the post, which would be marked, sent back and the next subject sent. Pressure and Flow of Fluids, Hydraulics, Hydrostatics, Pneumatics, The Science of Heat, Heating Systems, Hot Water Systems, Cold Water Systems, Ventilation, - just a few of the sections that come to mind. This all finished up with a final exam and a Diploma. It gave me all that I had been looking for.

Except for one thing. By this time, I was 25, I still had this problem with my health. Dr Bailey had frequently explained to me that my problem was septicaemia; poison was being generated somewhere in the body. He tried hard to trace it: teeth, water test for sugar, tonsils, but Dr Notley took one look at my tonsils and said quite positively, 'I am not taking those out, they are rotten,' and so it went on and on - tonsillitis, quinsy's, boils, carbuncles, nerve problems and on.

About this time Boughton Estates borrowed me, to help strip 20 tons of lead off the stables at Boughton House. We replaced the same area with 7 tons of 7 lb lead, which tells you how thick the old lead was. It was this job that was responsible for my interest in cast lead roof work, which we went on to do in quite a lot of churches and country houses in Northamptonshire.

My wife and I met, when we were 18, and I courted her until we were 26. Nora was 1 week older than me, her birthday was on

February 1st, mine on February 8th and we were married on 15th February 1941 in St Mary's Church.

By this time, she was teaching at St Mary's School, Fuller Street and she kept on teaching for the early years of our marriage. This was just as well, because in August of that year, I had a very bad car accident on a Sunday evening, August 17th and woke up three days later in the General Hospital with concussion, a broken femur and various other injuries. 8 months later, I left the hospital and started work, 53 weeks after the accident. I had received my call-up papers for the army, while I was in hospital. Eventually, they came again and I was placed in grade 3.

Shortly after this, I was sent to Lamport Hall, which had been used as an Italian prisoner-of-war accommodation, where they suspected an underground water leak. The water supply was from a large galvanised tank, that fed the whole house, and the water was pumped from a well in a field below the church, across the road. First, I had to prove whether or not there was a leak. So, I disconnected the delivery pipe and ran the pump and checked the delivery rate, which was about 800 gallons per hour.

I reconnected the delivery pipe, at the same time inserting a tee-piece with a pressure gauge in the branch, and ran the pump for one hour, having previously calculated the level and quantity of water in the tank. Of the 700 gallons pumped in one hour, only about 300 gallons reached the tank, which proved the leak.

Then I checked the gauge which registered 17 lb/in^2 pressure:

0.434 lb/in^2 per ft head = 2.3 ft head per lb/in^2,

gives 39.1 ft head to the leak.

My immediate reaction was that the leak must be up in the house, but this could not be, as there would be a lot of water in the house, which meant that it was somewhere up near the house. I started at the point of entry, where the water pipe came out of the ground, and started walking in a straight line towards the pump and well, across the drive and over a section of grass. I had progressed about 50 ft when I saw a slight depression in the grass. This continued for about 20 ft and then disappeared. They had given me two Italian prisoners to do any digging required, so I set one to work at the beginning of the suspected depression and the other 20 ft away. They both found the pipe about 1 ft 6 in deep, and both found a socket and they also found water. They dug towards each other and uncovered a 20 ft length of 1½ inch galvanised iron pipe, split from end to end.

The Ministry of Works men from Nottingham came to inspect the work, and were impressed by the way I had found the leak. They had a set of drawings on which they had to mark up all the plumbing and heating, and hot and cold supplies in the house, and they asked me if I could do this, so I earned myself another soft, but interesting job. But I enjoyed applying some of my knowledge of hydraulics to the job in hand. This estate and building are now looked after and run by English Heritage, and we have done further work there recently.

Shortly after this, Messrs George Knight, Builders, who we periodically worked for, had some work to carry out at Kimbolton Castle. The Castle had been taken over for the duration of the war by the Red Cross. The work in hand was to replace boarding and ceiling joists, to the lead covered roof. We had to remove the lead, so that the timber could be removed and replaced.

We duly removed the first section of lead, and Knights busied themselves repairing the woodwork. Another interesting fact relating to this particular section of roof was, that it was above the bedroom where Henry VIII imprisoned Catherine of Aragon.

The two army men in charge of Red Cross stores told us, that this room was locked and was supposed to have been locked and left as Catherine had left it, but they found a key from somewhere, and had opened the door and looked in. The cupboards were full of clothes falling to pieces with age.

While Knights were busy on the timber, we had to inspect and repair the rest of the roof as needed. It was a huge flat roof and kept us busy. This went on for several weeks, and then I had a letter from the War Ministry directing me to London. I had to report to Deptford Labour Exchange. I was given a rail ticket to London, where I was directed to work for John Laing, who was the main contractor for that area. I finally finished up in Charlton in lodgings, and also working in Charlton. The work consisted of nailing building paper over broken windows to keep them habitable.

This was the period of the V1 and V2 rockets. We were sleeping on the floor under the protection of a Morrison shelter, which was a large, heavy-gauge steel table. The rockets came over at about 7.30 - 8.00 a.m. and again at mid-day and about 5.00 p.m. One day, we had been covering broken windows on a block of flats, and left off at 5.00 p.m. and were walking home. I remember a man was putting a front door on again. We stopped to talk to him, and I remember his words to this day, 'This ... door knows its way, on and off its hinges.' Just after we left him, the V1s started coming over; there were three of them close together. We watched them to see what they were going to do. One cut out and dived straight on to the flats, that we had just left. As soon as one cut out, as in this instance, everyone dropped flat, where they stood.

One went on and dropped somewhere near the river; the third one went on and we heard the engine eventually cut out, but no explosion, so eventually, we reached home. Just before we reached home, there was an almighty bang, not too far away. We were told later, this third bomb had cut out, but had glided straight, turned round and glided back and finally dropped on Lewisham market, just when all the locals were doing their evening shopping. Approximately, 150 people were killed.

This went on for about one month, and then our foreman handed me a letter which instructed me to report to Deptford

Labour Exchange once again. The official at the Labour Exchange started berating me, and shouting at me 'What do you mean by leaving your job at Kimbolton?' to which I replied, when I could get a word in, 'My wife is expecting her first baby. I was directed here; you don't suppose I came to this Hell Hole by choice, do you?' or something like that. After which he cooled down and said 'Anyway, here is your rail ticket back to Kettering; report back to Kimbolton tomorrow.' I said 'thank you very much' and caught the first train home. But believe me, it was a Hell Hole at that time. The poor women; a young married woman had tuberculosis very badly, where we were lodging.

We went back to Kimbolton where Knights had finished their woodwork, and we replaced the lead and finished our lead burning repairs on the roof. After London, it was like heaven - so peaceful and quiet.

There were a lot of wild strawberries in the park, and we used to fill our lunch boxes with strawberries. Also, when Knights ran out of petrol (petrol was rationed) we caught the Cambridge train and walked across the fields, about 2 miles, to Kimbolton and back again at night. When this happened, we used to pick blackberries and mushrooms. How lucky I was to get back to Kimbolton.

After this, I was working at Wyton Aerodrome, near Huntingdon. This was quite interesting; it was a very large Pathfinder Lancaster base with Mosquito night operation flight also.

We were working on a new NAAFI site for the main contractor, Thackray of Huntingdon. I had an apprentice with me, and we used to catch a bus to Huntingdon on Sunday evening, getting off the bus in Huntingdon, and walking up the Hartford Road, towards Wyton. Another bus from Huntingdon to Wyton would come along, which we used to get on when it came.

One night, we walked as far as Hartford and I had a very bad cold, so while the apprentice kept his eye open for the bus, I went into the pub, and bought a quick whisky and as he was serving me, my assistant shouted 'Bus!'. I quickly drank the whisky and handed the landlord a £1 note and ran for the door, but stopped quickly, and went back to the landlord and said 'what about the 10/- note' all in a loud voice, so that everyone in the bar could clearly hear it. The landlord opened his other hand, disclosing a ten-shilling note. Having collected my proper change, I caught the bus. His regular customers in the bar would be watching their change in future! The other thing about this story is, that we still had then 10/- and £1 notes, and also the price of a glass of whisky was something less than 10/- (ten shillings).

This was late 1943 or early 1944, towards the end of the war, and I remember the first raid on Berlin. The planes were arriving back at about 8.00 a.m., and everybody was counting the planes as they landed. One was missing. Sometimes, a damaged plane was late getting back, but time went by and no sign of the missing Lancaster, and then at about 9.30 a.m., back it came, only one of its four engines working.

While I was there, there were many similar experiences. A little further down the North Road was an American Air Base, Alconbury, and this was a Flying Fortress base. Thackrays were also doing work there, and our foreman was also in charge of this work. They used to carry out daylight raids, and used to go out and return over Wyton and sometimes, they used to come back the worse for wear. We used to watch them come back, and one day one came over with its large tailplane lying flat, and in the middle of the fuselage a huge hole, so big that from the ground it appeared to be in two pieces. Some of the four engines were out of action.

The foreman happened to be on site when it landed. I think they carried 13 crew, and he told us that the ground staff talked him down and it landed safely, landed by the one man remaining alive in the aircraft, and he was not a pilot. They had suffered a direct hit.

Another instance was on a Friday night at about 4.00 p.m. The overnight raids took off at about this time, and I remember Thackray's men were queuing at the office for their wages, when suddenly there was a terrific 'Bang!' and the ground shook like a piece of jelly. Eventually, we were told that one of the Lancasters was about to take off with a full complement of bombs, when the flight engineer detected a fault on a photographic flare. It was a cold winter night and fortunately, the crew decided to take cover in a Nissen shelter near the dispersal site, while the flight engineer dealt with the faulty flare. The next thing they knew was, the fully-loaded plane blew up. It demolished a house the other side of the road, and great chunks of concrete from the dispersal point were blown half-way across a field over the road.

One morning, when we arrived on the site where we were working, a Lancaster lay on its back in the next field with its tail sticking through the hedge of our site. No doubt, the wireless report that morning would say 'All our planes returned safely'; perhaps they did, but some of them were so badly knocked about, that they could not land safely.

We used to get our mid-day meals at the old NAAFI on the aerodrome, and here we would pick up the latest stories and news of raids and stories of interest, from the RAF personnel and other workers. One such story was that the night before, the Mosquitoes had returned from the raid, and one of the planes that came back with them had attacked the aerodrome, and shot up the landing planes and then cleared off. An enterprising, young German had joined them somewhere on the way back, and attacked them as they landed. Miraculously, no damage was done, apart from the odd bullet hole in an aircraft here and there; a ground staff WAAF was injured slightly, and they found a dead rabbit which had been shot.

One of the pilot officers used to come into the NAAFI for a cup of tea and a bun whatever; his face was one huge, horrible scar, holes where ears, eyes, nose and mouth used to be. Whatever the incident was, it must have been a considerable time before I saw him, because his face was completely healed and some hospital had done a very good job on his face and on him. He looked very fit, upright and healthy until you looked back at his face; it also looked as if he was operational again.

Most of the men in our Nissen hut sleeping accommodation were like me, young married men, downgraded and no use for active service, but there were two men who normally were friends and used to work together, one a red-headed large Irishman and the other a Cockney. They were a bit loud and nobody had much time or association with them. We had all gone to bed and were just off to sleep, when we were all awakened by a commotion outside and then the door burst open. The big Irishman picked another man up and hit him, and knocked him flying into the room. They were the two friends who had been into Huntingdon drinking and had fallen out and had a drunken argument outside. Anyhow, he picked the Cockney up again and hit him again, and repeated this performance all round the room and nobody interfered, until he reached us and hitting him again, he landed on my mate's bed. I jumped out of bed and said, 'Get out and take your fight somewhere else.' Surprisingly, he dragged his unfortunate friend outside and did exactly as I commanded, and took their fight somewhere else. The next day he, the less fortunate one, was in the Huntingdon General Hospital, and the police were looking for his 'friend'.

One weekend, we returned on the Sunday evening and there had been fun and games over the weekend. At that time, just in front of the main entrance to Wyton aerodrome, there were some tennis courts. To our surprise, there was a large bomb crater in the centre of one court. We were later informed that one of the Flying Fortresses was returning to Alconbury, and was in some sort of trouble. He still had some bombs on board, and had to get rid of them before landing, and dropped them on Wyton aerodrome. On the face of it, this seemed a terrible thing to do, but looking back over the foregoing stories I have already related, and not knowing the state of the Fortress or its crew, we or anyone else could not criticise their actions, but several bombs were jettisoned. It was fortunate that they missed the bomb dump, just over the road, from Huntingdon. The stories go on and on, but one thing is certain, only the crews of these aircraft knew the horrors they had to face.

Shortly after this, the war ended and we all returned to our normal lives and in November 1945, I started my business. I was now 30 years of age, happily married with one son, David. Shortly after I started, I was troubled with my health problems; I had shortly before this been told that I had a fistula, and would have to have an operation. But there were no beds available; 18 months later I began to lose weight: 2 stone in 2 weeks, and at the same time an awful smell developed, which was strangely familiar to me, and then I remembered where I had experienced this smell before: the Buccleuch Ward, Kettering General Hospital, when a man lost his leg with gangrene. I immediately dragged myself to the doctors. He said, 'let me look,' but he did not need to look, he would have known without looking. However, he said 'Good God, how long have you been like this?' and without waiting for an answer, he instructed me to be at the hospital at 9.00 a.m. the next morning, where he immediately operated. He came to me after the operation with a face as long as a fiddle, and said he had done his best, and he hoped that he had got it all away. But I think he must have done a good job, as I am still here 85 years of age, but it did leave a bit of irritation until I turned 60. After the operation, I looked at the report sheet which read 'anal fissure', not a fistula, the same area. This puzzled me for a short time, a split in the back passage, then I remembered the splinter when I was 4 years old. All those years of trouble from a splinter.

I kept on with my weekly dose of laxative until eventually, at the age sometime in my 60s, I realised the irritation had finally gone. After the operation, my health quickly improved, which was good, because I quickly built up the business and was able to enjoy work and life in general.

First of all, I operated from a lock-up garage in Clarke & Hobbs bottom yard, where they made tile fireplaces, but I quickly needed larger premises. One day, I was working at a Mrs Wilmot's, 17 Broadway, and as I worked, I was chatting away with Mrs Wilmot, and she asked me how I was progressing. I told her I was getting on well, the business was growing, but I needed larger premises to work from. She said, 'Go and see Paul (her husband); he has a yard for sale.' So as soon as I finished the work, I went straight up to Wilmot's Laundry, next to the Rectory in Church Walk. I rang the doorbell, and Paul himself appeared at the door. He said, 'Hello Boy, what do you want?'

I replied, 'You have a yard for sale.'

He said, 'Yes, Boy.'

I said, 'How much?'

He said, 'Twelve hundred.'

I said, 'One thousand,' and he said 'Eleven hundred.' I said okay, and so in the space of one minute, I had bought myself a yard for eleven hundred pounds, which I did not have. But the premises were perfect for our requirements, so I thought very quickly, went and saw the people with whom I had a small mortgage on my house in Roundhill Road. Since moving in, in lieu of a bad debt, a good friend of mine had decorated the house right through and prior to this, I had centrally-heated the house. The mortgage people took a quick look, and immediately extended the mortgage to £1400 and gave me a cheque for £1000.00, which I passed on to Mr Wilmot the same day and the yard was mine.

The next day we were carrying our bits of stock from Clarke & Hobbs yard next door, when the Regimental Sergeant Major from the Drill Hall next door came out, looking a bit puzzled and eventually said, 'What are you doing?' I replied, 'We are just moving in; I bought this yesterday' and he replied, 'Well b--- me. We've got a cheque in the post for this yard.' So, without having the slightest idea of this, we had 'gazumped' and by a short head had obtained a very useful premises. We have just vacated these premises after 50 years trading, and moved to new premises in Garrard Way on the Telford Estate - 50 happy and successful years. I never did find out what the other cheque was for, but guessing I think that the T.A. cheque was probably for £1000.

While we were in Clarke & Hobbs yard, we were having difficulty in getting copper tube because all building materials were strictly rationed, and everyone had to send coupons with orders. Before I started my business, I used to send for catalogues from all sorts of firms, purely to extend my knowledge. One of these, Builders Copper Tube Ltd, came to mind. I was desperate, so I thought, well, they can only refuse the order, so I sent for 1 ton of copper tube, mixed sizes and was very surprised when 1 ton arrived, no questions about licences. The only problem was that the whole ton was in 20 ft lengths, which of course would not go into the garage. So, we put it in the roof of a shed covering fireplace back firebricks. A taxi service, Jean's Taxis, were also using this yard at the time, so the yard was open all night. But nobody touched the tube, but today it would not be safe for one night. Clarke & Hobbs were having trouble getting copper tube and were buying it off me.

The new premises solved all these problems, but much later we had several break-ins, and lost all our stock of tube on several occasions.

As things progressed, we, in the early days, needed a phone and we were having a problem getting a line. While we were going through this problem, we did some work for a certain customer and he told me that he had just had the phone installed. Just after we had done his work, we were warned that he did not pay his bills. So, I quickly pressed for payment. He said that if I met him in School Lane at 5 p.m. on Friday night, he would pay me. I duly arrived as arranged, but he did not turn up.

I thought quick and hard, thinking I shall have to chase this man or no money. Then I remembered the new telephone line from the post in Roundhill Road, and knew that he had a bungalow prefab in the Highfield Road estate. So, I went to the telephone post and sure enough there was a bright new shining copper wire, which I followed; it dipped down to a bungalow. I rang the bell and he came to the door and was so surprised, that he paid me there and then. Naturally, I did no more work for him.

In those early days, my parents were very supportive; business was good and moving forward quickly and we were managing with 2 hand trucks, but we needed transport, so I put in a tender of £80 for a Post Office vehicle and a postman showed me the vehicle and asked me what it was worth, and I said not more than £80. The postman had it for £85. Well, you live and learn. The next one was at Wellingborough Post Office, and went through the same procedure, but when the postman showed me the vehicle and asked the question, I said that it was not worth more than £50. I put in a tender of £85 and obtained my first van. It had done 117,000 miles and was on its 4th engine, and we eventually completed about 400,000 miles with it until it developed a leak in the radiator. We could not get another Morris Minor radiator and no-one else would drive it, because the steering was so bad: one complete turn of the steering wheel before any steering was felt, so we sold it for £10.00 to Arthur Heath. My parents, I think, paid for this.

My wife Nora was also very supportive and quietly, but very positively, gave me support and encouragement. When I was in hospital for 8 months in 1941, she came up every evening in all weathers to see me, and after this, all through my years of running the business, she supported and helped whenever she could, filling in when the office staff were ill or had left, etc. I was very lucky with my wife and parents; I received their support and help whenever it was needed.

Shortly before I started my business about 1935, I was working on a farm belonging to Boughton Estates, situated near the Warkton, Grafton, Cranford, Twywell crossroads. We were putting a 2-inch cast-iron water supply to the farm in preparation for a new tenant moving into the farm. The estate workers told me of an interesting incident, shortly before I arrived. The Boughton Estates had just bought their first tractor, and they appointed their past ploughman to learn how to use the tractor, having spent all his life with horses, to plough the fields. The people supplying the tractor demonstrated the handling of the machine, and sat with him on the tractor up and down the field a few times, and then let him have a go by himself. He did very well until he reached the bottom of the field, and then he panicked and forgot all the instructions and stood up and shouted 'Wo you B---, Wo!' The poor new tractor did not understand and kept straight on, through the hedge and into the ditch. Any good horse would have understood and immediately, would have responded. So much for modern machinery!

Many years later, there was a fortunate follow-up to my working on this farm. Eventually, we finished our work on the farm and the new tenant moved in - a Scotsman, Mr Meyer and his wife, and a daughter and a son, Billy Meyer, all very nice people, whom I got to know very well. Billy was about 14 years of age.

About 25-30 years later, we were in the habit of going over to Twywell every Thursday evening, having a quiet game of skittles and a moderate drink, and on our way home on one occasion, it was very foggy and approaching the cross-roads I missed the sign warning of a double bend, and too late I was on the bend and shouted to my passengers, 'Hang on,' and ran on to the grass verge, with our front wheels firmly embedded in a manure heap, but otherwise, no damage. If I had tried to take the bend, I would certainly have turned over, which would probably have damaged the car and its occupants.

Anyhow, it was obvious as it was November and lots of mud about, apart from the manure, it was obvious we were not going to get the car back on the road, and it was about 11 p.m. and perhaps a bit later, so we had decided to start walking when a cyclist came round the bend towards us, and he shouted, 'Are you alright?' I immediately recognised the voice and I shouted in reply, 'Billy Meyer' and he replied, 'That's right, who is that?' to which I replied, 'Fred Blount'. He said, 'Hang on, I will be back in about ten minutes with a tractor.' Sure enough, we could hear the tractor coming, but could not see it because it had no lights. He hooked a chain on to the front axle and out we came. How lucky can you get?

He afterwards explained that he was going to the farm; his father, who by now was an old man, was very ill and he was going to sit with him overnight. But certainly, this was a fine example of a good friend in the right place at the right time.

These trips to Twywell went on for some years, and a number of incidents happened on our way back.

On another of these occasions, we were coming back through Warkton and approaching the bridge over the River Ise, and another car was coming from the opposite direction and as he crossed over the bridge, he put his lights up on main beam and immediately, I saw a man lying on the road. I jammed on the brakes, and stopped about 2 feet away from the body on the road.

He turned out to be a local character, who was on his way home from the Warkton Club, well and truly drunk, he lay on the road and his bike was on the top of the hedge. I thanked the other motorist for his quick action. If we had run over the man, even though he was drunk, it would have been difficult for me. We rang for the ambulance, and they took him off to Kettering General Hospital.

On another occasion, we were approaching the double bend on the top end of Warkton, when we commented on two beams of light pointing up into the night sky; it was a frosty night, but we negotiated both bends and never felt a thing, but when we reached the lights, it was a car back end in the ditch in a vertical position. The driver said he had skidded on ice, as we subsequently found out. After some difficulty, we managed to open the driver's door and up to this not a sound from the car, but as we finally got the door opened, screams came from the back seat. There were four occupants, the driver was lying there still smoking a pipe, and one of the three ladies was heavily pregnant. We quickly drove on, and phoned for an ambulance, which quickly came and sorted them out, but with the position of the car, it must have been very difficult.

Fred Blount

April 2000

Fred Blount Memoirs 3

R.F. Blount
My Work as a Plumber and Heating Engineer - Part 2

In November 1945, I started my business as a plumber and heating engineer. I was intent on making a success of this new venture, and spent every minute from early morning until 12 midnight and after on some occasions, except Thursday evenings and Saturday afternoons and Sundays; weekends I reserved to spend with my wife and later, also my children.

I remember one Saturday; the phone rang just as I was leaving with my wife. Foolishly, I picked up the phone and a strange voice said, "Can you help me? I have a blocked drain. I have been trying to free it, all Monday evening, Tuesday evening, Wednesday, Thursday, Friday and all this morning, Saturday [now 2.30 p.m.]." Now, I am a reasonable man and ready to help any reasonable fellow citizen, but this to me was a bit too much, Monday to Saturday, so I politely told him to keep going and I was sure he would succeed eventually.

On Thursday evenings, myself and some of my friends went out to one of the neighbouring villages, and had a game of skittles or darts and a moderate drink. In the early days, it was Geddington and later Cranford and then Twywell.

The road to Twywell and back

In the early days, I used to pick up my friend Jack Payne. Jack and I went back a long way, from 1922-1923 when Jack was a server and I was in the choir at St Mary's Church, in the days of Father Glaister and apart from the war years, spent one evening a week out together somewhere.

By this time, about 1950, Jack had built a house in Geddington, and I used to pick him up along with two other friends, Frank Bryan and Sid Read, both of them gents' hairdressers and tobacconists and we made our way to Twywell via the road to Grafton Underwood. As we passed the back of Boughton House, four full-grown deer ran in front of us and I had to brake hard to avoid hitting them and every one said, "One of those would have been good for Christmas." It was a week or so before Christmas.

We reached the cross-roads to Cranford, Twywell and Kettering, where we were stopped by the police, who politely asked if they could look inside the vehicle, which they did and immediately recognised Sid as his barber.

He explained that they were looking for poultry thieves. What a pity that we did not have a dead deer in the back - it would have made their evening!

It was about this same time and the same road but on this occasion, Grafton Underwood was flooded and the residents were standing on their doorsteps, obviously concerned regarding the water coming indoors. Also at this time, contractors were laying a main sewage system in the village and a large deep trench was in existence, also full of water, making driving dangerous. We made our way carefully through the floods and eventually arrived at Twywell.

Later, we made our way home by the same route through the floods and approaching a bend in the road at the back of Boughton Estates, I applied my brakes for the bend, only to find I had no brakes and I finished up in the ditch, luckily landing softly on our side on the hedge. It was about 11 o'clock. Jack ran along to Geddington and phoned up an all-night service garage, who came and pulled us out.

Again, on our way to Twywell one late spring evening, Frank Bryan, who was always interested in wild birds, spotted an owl flying into a hole in a tree at the side of the road, so we stopped while he went to investigate. I have heard of people who invade their nests, getting attacked by birds, especially when they have young ones, but this one did much better, it relieved itself all over his face and down his jacket.

Shortly after this we were returning home from Twywell, it was after dark, and in the headlights and on the road was an owl. We stopped the car, and Frank again approached the bird. It did not move until he reached out to pick it up, and then it flew away. I wonder if this was the same bird or one of its offsprings.

1934 was a year when many memorable things happened in my life that were going to influence the rest of my working life. I was 19 years of age and there was talk of our boss at W. Burton & Sons, the son-in-law, retiring and the firm winding up at the end of the year. He was not enjoying the best of health and by this time he had built a house and corner shop at the bottom of St Peters Avenue, the shop was a small general store and sweet shop.

Horace Toseland was his name and he had run the business of Plumbing & Heating successfully for many years, under difficulty with his health and I always found him to be a good man to work for.

In the August of 1934, Tommy Capps borrowed me for two weeks to complete a plumbing and heating job at Ferndale, 17 The Headlands, while he was away getting married and on honeymoon. Mr Thompson, Solicitor of Market Street, had bought the house, which he and his wife and family moved into, when we had completed our work. Tommy was busy and I was looking for a job, so I stayed there until 1945, when I started my own business.

Shortly after we finished at Ferndale, Boughton Estates borrowed me from J.T. Capps to assist with the leadwork on the restoration of the Stable Block adjoining Boughton House, where we removed approx. 20 tons of old cast lead and recovered the same area with approx. 7 tons of new 7 lb cast lead. This gives you some idea of the thickness of the old lead, which was probably the original lead, which would have been cast on site on a prepared sand bed. I was helping the estate plumber Teddy Burleigh, who shortly before this, had been employed by the Co-operative Builders of Havelock Street, Kettering, and that man could turn a piece of sheet lead inside out. I learned a lot from him about leadwork, and carried out a great deal of cast leadwork on churches and country houses in Northamptonshire.

The stables used to house the Duke's private collection of timber, oak mostly, cut in different ways, quartered and otherwise to produce beautiful grain effects. This and forestry, I believe, was his special interest.

The roof was mainly covered with slates. The roof was composed of two gables with a large lead gutter between the gables. The inside of the gables was blue slate, which would be copper or galvanised iron nailed and carried out by 'Cowboy' York and his brother, slating contractors, who lived in School Lane, Kettering, and the outside of the gables were covered with Collyweston slate, secured with wooden pegs, to match the house roof. Mr Knapp of Collyweston did this part of the roof.

I was there several months; we had to be there at 7.30 a.m. before it was properly daylight in the mid-winter, and often it would be 9.00 a.m. before we were on the roof; this was a new experience for me, as in the town it was a much tighter schedule.

Teddy Burleigh had spent his younger days in the Leicester area where he attended Leicester Tech. and at this time, I was looking for technical training, but there were no Technical Schools dealing with plumbing or heating in Northamptonshire. Much later, Wellingborough had Tech and a plumbing section, which I attended and picked up lead burning and previous to this, I did a 4-year correspondence course, which alongside my daily work, kept me on my feet. Incidentally, the 4-year course took me 6 years to complete, but it was well worthwhile.

During wet weather, we had to fill in our time assisting in the Boughton House, preparing valuables for transport to the British Museum.

Some of the names of the men I worked with on the estate were Yankee Toseland of Geddington, Mr West of Warkton, one of the Clipston brothers of Geddington.

1934

I used to go to the outdoor swimming baths at this time, before I went to work and right through the winter, sometimes a quick dive and across the width and back, back to the cubicle, turn round and see your frozen footmarks on the concrete. I have a photo of an early morning group showing the baths covered in 6 inches of ice, except where Mr White had broken us a hole, big enough to dive in and up the steps quickly. But this all came to an end in early March 1935, because we had had no rain since the previous April 1934. Cransley and Thorpe Malsor reservoirs were both empty, and by this time we were existing on water carefully rationed from the Wicksteed Lake and Mr Duce, the then Sanitary Inspector, declared the baths closed, as the water was unfit for us to go in. It had not been changed for about 6 months. Henry Billson was also one of the early morning swimmers, also Ike Bates and his friend Alfy Haigh. Ike was teaching Alf to swim and on the Boxing Day when the Evening Telegraph took the photo, Mr White had broken the ice by the steps at the 3 ft end, and Alfy used to walk down one step at a time. This used to kill us to watch him, it was shock enough to dive in and out at the deep end. Happy Days.

Eventually, it started to rain at the end of March, and we returned to normal with the water problem.

A temporary 6" cast-iron water main was laid in the gutters from Wicksteed Lake, up London Road, Windmill Avenue, Avondale Road and on up to Clover Hill by the Pleasure Park, where there was at that time a Water Tower which in the past had gravity-fed all Kettering and later a pumped supply. But it saved all Kettering from dying of thirst.

Some years later we were working at Ferndale once again. We were called in to sweep the boiler house chimney. When we installed the heating, we fitted a new gas boiler. Since that time, all gas boiler flues are always lined with a flexible steel liner to avoid condensation problems. By this time, condensation was already damaging the decoration in rooms above.

Anyway, we put the rods up the chimney and when I thought we had enough rods in, I sent my mate, Bill Moore of Geddington, out to see if the brush was through the pot. He came back and said, "No, it had not come through yet." So, I put some more rods on and repeated the process. Again, no brush, more rods and again, no brush. By this time, I was running out of rods and there was obviously something wrong, so I went out to see for myself. Sure enough, there was no brush out of the pot, but while we stood there looking up at the chimney, something caught my eye lower down, and waving up and down inside a bedroom window was the brush with a ladies' dress hanging on it. We hurried up the stairs to the bedroom, to find that there was a flue access plate on the side of the chimney breast; the recess had been made into a cupboard, the rods had pushed off the access plate, collected a dress and gone right round the bedroom and finished up hanging in front of the window. On its way round the room, it had left sooty marks on the wallpaper. We finished the sweeping of the chimney and no doubt, Tommy had to settle with Mrs Thompson via his insurance company.

Eventually, Mr Thompson died and I still did work for Mrs Thompson, who had some flats built at the top of the garden, which bordered on Bowling Green Avenue. She was always very pleasant and saw the funny side of the chimney-sweeping episode.

The NCC bought the house and turned it into an old people's home, where we again did a lot of work over the years.

My eldest son David has a bungalow in Brittany, where we have two weeks' summer holiday every year. My daughter Margaret and I were returning from one of these holidays 5 or 6 years ago, about 1994, and coming back from Plymouth, we came through Stow on the Wold, where we stopped for refreshment and went into an antique shop with a café upstairs.

A man came to serve us and eventually he said, "Where do you come from?" I said "Kettering," to which he replied, "I thought I recognised the dialect. I too come from Kettering." We exchanged names and his name was Thompson and eventually, it became clear that he was Mr Thompson, the solicitor of Ferndale's son. He explained that he joined the regular army and had retired and was living in Stow, pursuing his interest in antiques. I asked him if he remembered calling in at Ferndale, and catching us filling our lunch bags with William pears from the orchard. He was at the Grammar School in Bowling Green Road, now the Council Offices.

After this we had a long talk about Kettering, and some of his friends and residents of the town.

St Mary's Scouts

As I have already indicated, my wife and I were living in Princes Street/Tresham Street and we both from childhood, were taken to St Mary's Church, until we were married and moved to Roundhill Road.

From the age of about 9, I joined the St Mary's Scouts. Our Scout Masters were Obid Bye and Ray Knight. When I was about 16-17, the troop fizzled out and by this time, Claud Harvey, who was for some time headmaster at St Mary's School, started a St Mary's School troop, so we attached ourselves to them for the annual camp.

The first year that we exercised this arrangement, we went to Heacham on the east coast, and on the Thursday evening it was our turn to cook the evening meal. There were 3 or 4 of us from the Church troop, perhaps too many of us, too many cooks and all that; anyway, all the rest had gone to the pictures in Hunstanton, about 20 of them. Everything was fine until someone carelessly knocked the dixie off the Primus stove. We quickly scraped up the vegetables and all that we could recover, including some grass, but we had lost most of the gravy. Panic stations, 20 hungry scouts coming back to this. However, we went and raided the stores at the back of the tent. It was getting towards the end of the holiday, so there was not a lot left, but first we found 7 or 8 Symington soups, and then a fair quantity of cheese cut into cubes, some vegetables, and then we struck gold, about 2 lbs of bacon; unfortunately the flies had got at it, and it was heaving with maggots. Well, we were desperate, so all these treasures we dumped into the dixie and the whole lot topped up with water and once again got it bubbling away, and then we tried it and were very pleasantly surprised - it tasted good.

Eventually, everyone returned for supper and they all wanted more and more, so everything turned out very well. There was only one awkward so-and-so, wanted to know what the white bits were in the gravy. We could not tell them it was maggots - they enjoyed it. Thinking quickly, we told them it was rice.

The following year, they went to Dawlish, which was a catastrophe. Myself, and Bill Newbold and our girls (we had both started courting) were in lodgings in Dawlish. One night there was a terrific storm. It was so bad, that when we eventually went out all the storm water manholes were off, and water coming out like a 2 ft diameter fountain and water everywhere, finding its way into the sea.

We decided to go to the camp to see how they had fared. They were completely washed out and had bolted into a cricket pavilion in the adjoining field. All their kit was soaked, knives, forks and spoons were buried in a sea of mud. We all stopped and helped them clear up.

The following day we decided to go to Torquay by train. We had to get out at Torr station and walk the rest, as the railway embankment had been swept away by flood. When we arrived in Torquay, all the beautiful gardens, which the town is famed for, were drifts of earth on the roads, the deck chairs were all floating in the sea. What a storm!

Some years later, a similar storm at Lynton and Lynmouth changed the course of the River Lyn, sweeping whole houses away that were in the way of the new water course.

Churchwarden

During my term of office as Churchwarden with Ken Bacon, the Tower Captain repaired or renewed the bell housings and re-hung the bells in 1979. The Tower Captain at that time was Jim Mossop, ably assisted by Mr Derek Sibson and Mr Peter Fleckney. I think that Mr Fleckney was a pattern maker in a foundry. I am not sure about that, but he was very good with woodwork and did a good job. It was a major operation at the time; he also carved the oak handrail on the steps near the lectern to the Sawyer Chapel. Other Bellringers also assisted.

Also at this time, two more treble bells were added to the top of the peal. These were ordered and cast by Taylor's of Loughborough; one was cast with Ken's name on it and the other with my name on it. We were both invited to spend a day at Taylor's with a conducted tour of the foundry.

When we carried out work on the new north aisle roof, one sheet was cast with the Church Wardens' names on the sheets, somewhere near the middle of the roof. The Wardens' names were Walter Pringle and Frank Valentine. Walter was headmaster at St Mary's Church of England Primary School in Burton Latimer, and Frank was at this time with the Kettering Rural Council as Assistant Surveyor. Shortly after this, he moved to Daventry District Council as Chief Surveyor.

It was also about this time when the national water boards altered the water regulations to ban the use of lead pipes for drinking water supplies, because in soft water areas, especially the acid in soft water areas, usually associated with peat soil areas, has a solvent action on the lead and in the long-term causes lead poisoning, for which there is no cure.

After this, in all specifications for new work, the plumbing section would commence with the passage 'Remove all existing lead pipes and replace with copper or P.V.C. pipe'.

We had sophisticated air traffic, space travel to the moon and other planets, but it had taken 2000 years of civilisation to get rid of lead, for drinking water distribution.

In this area, the water is naturally hard, and is treated at the reservoirs and water-treatment plants to a suitable degree of hardness, but in some areas, it can be very dangerous.

I was made aware of this at an early age, when I was 16 years old, I started taking the Plumbing Trade Journal and one of these early publications told the story of a young doctor, fresh from medical school, who joined a practice in Chester and having his recent training fresh in his mind, quickly realised that a lot of his patients were suffering from similar stomach complaints and symptoms. He did a series of tests, and found that he had over 300 cases of advanced lead poisoning on his panel of patients.

So, approximately 40 years on after I read this article something is eventually being done. We are very slow to move, but we get there in time. But it is like the asbestos problem; there are many miles/tons of lead water service buried underground as there is asbestos; asbestos within eyesight almost everywhere you stop and look around, but we are slowly moving in the right directions as we should, because both these items have been real killers and health hazards.

Fred Blount
June 2000
Fred Blount Memoirs 4

R.F. Blount

More on the Church and its Surrounding Buildings

When I first started in work at the age of 14, Easter 1929, there was a row of buildings backing on to the drive of Kettering Parish Church of St Peter & Paul, starting at the top end from the North Gates in a straight building line down to the pavement. The top premises were the Kettering Water Board Offices (Water Inspector, Mr Evers), where I, from time to time, fetched water meters that we had to fit, usually to business premises; next to this were the offices of Berry Brothers & Bagshaw, Estate Agents, and then came the premises of Paynes, Bakers & Confectioners, and then the bottom block in line with the front gates of the church was 'The Albion Temperance Hotel'. The main interest for us young hopeful billiards players at that time, was the billiard table with real ivory balls. You will notice that at this time it was billiards not snooker, which was the fashionable game; snooker did not become popular until after the Second World War. At this time there was a right of way to the Rectory through the centre of the Market Place. This has recently been redirected with the reconstruction of the Market Place, in the year 2000 to the church side of the Market Place, roughly in line with the old, front building line of the buildings described above. At the top of the Market Place is the rectory wall adjacent to the North Church Gates and Church Walk. This wall still marks the boundary to the new Rectory, just completed this year. Immediately next to the old Rectory Gates, is the Parish Hall.

The Parish Hall when first built was probably one of the first schools in Kettering and forerunner to the Parish Church School in the Horsemarket. The Head Teacher was Miss Shayler. Another school about the same time was the British School in School Lane, later, in my time, used as a woodwork centre under the watchful eye of Mr Arber and his assistant Owen Mason.

The old Parish Church School stands more or less as it was built, of a local iron or sandstone; internally various alterations have been made from time to time, to make it more useful as a Parish Room and to suit its various functions for parties, concerts and for the various sales and money-raising events. At times, it is too small for our requirements and, looking to the future, several schemes have been put forward and considered to enlarge the Hall.

The North Door of the church is interesting, as are all other parts of the building, but the North Door has a small room above it where, going back to the 1300s, and according to some old records, the priest-in-charge used to occupy this old room, access being gained by way of a door and stone staircase to the right of the entrance door into the church. There are narrow slit apertures, whereby he could look out over the Market Place, to see anyone approaching the church who might have required his services. Much later, a rectory was built, but in those early days, the job was not very attractive, more like the life of a hermit.

Also, above the North Door there are two niches and some years ago, Jim Carr did some research and found out that they used to house a carving of St Peter and the other St Paul. He then carved two figures from a stone window sill from a terrace house pulled down in an old part of the town. When completed, he placed them in the niches and enhanced the appearance of the North Door.

There is not a lot of recorded history of the church before 1650 as, according to records, most of the history and records were written in Latin and a change to English was made about 1650.

Kettering about this time had a visitation of the plague and in 1665, there are recordings of burials with the letters Pl after the name, indicating that they had died of the plague.

Most of the town's business at this time was conducted in or at the Vestry Meetings, such things as disposal of collections of household rubbish accumulated outside front doors, repairs to the church fabric and, in 1756, the supplying of the first church clock in the tower by Thomas Eayre for a sum not exceeding £60.00. Also, the churchwardens took a leading part in these Vestry Meetings, dealing with the poor and health matters in the town, along with other leading characters and business men of the town, Richard Stockburn and Sawyer.

Apparently, also at this time, market business was conducted in part of the church, also a fire engine was housed somewhere on the church precincts, but was moved to Lower Street about 1780. Thos. Eayre had a bell foundry near Wadcroft until it was pulled down very recently, in a clearance for a car park behind Woolworths. It is also interesting, the name Wadcroft, which again was part of old Kettering with stone cottages and cleared when the P.O. was built, was originally Woadcroft, getting its name from the meadow below where woad was to be found, dating back to the days of the wool industry, using woad for dyeing. All these old, historic parts of Kettering have now disappeared in the name of progress (?).

The Parish Church, with the development of the Boot & Shoe Trade, Leather Dressing, and Clothing Trades and the inevitable growth of the town, had to provide for the religious development also, and built daughter churches in each parish, mostly corrugated-iron structures, some of which still exist and are regularly attended and well attended, our own St Michael's Church being the finest surviving example.

St Mary's was one of the early corrugated iron churches, replaced about 1900 with a fine permanent building, the priest-in-charge being Fr Glaister. I myself was brought up here. I had six maiden aunts who saw to it that my Christian teaching was taken care of from an early age. When I was 8, I joined the choir and the Scouts; at the age of 14-15, I became a server and continued until after we were married at St Mary's, on 15th February, 1941. In 1945, we moved to Roundhill Road where, shortly after, I started in business and for two or three years I concentrated on building up the business, but eventually with the children, we came to the Parish Church via St Michael's Church.

All Saints' Church was also a corrugated-iron church. I remember attending the consecration service of the new chancel and altar as a choir boy or server, I am not sure which, but it could have been about 1930. Fr Round was the priest-in-charge at this time. Part of the old building was left standing, with plans to complete the church and add a nave when funds were available.

But by this time, between the wars, the good old days were over, when every street had its thriving shoe factory, the owners of which were generously supporting all the town churches and all other amenities, so I think All Saints' are still managing without the nave.

The other daughter church closely connected to St Peter & Paul was St Luke's in Alexandra Street, where in 1920 & 30, Fr Kingdom, who was an assistant priest at St Peter & Paul, was priest-in-charge at St Luke's. I remember this church more for its Saturday evening social events and dancing classes run by Mrs Cooper, Fr Cooper's wife of St Mary's Church at this time; looking back, these lettings were a desperate effort to keep the church going, but it gradually went downhill and was eventually sold, I think as a builder's yard.

Another church, which I never did know much about, was St Phillip's. I remember this again for its social functions and dances in the 1930s. It was situated somewhere in the Union St/Field St area, but that too seems to have disappeared.

The other one we all know very well is our own St Michael's Church. A lot could be written about its progress and support over the years, but it is so closely connected to St Peter & Paul, that there is little I can write that you do not already know, except perhaps that I do miss our old mutual friend Eric Torbell, who did so much work for St Michael's, St Peter & Paul and the Pensioners' Parliament. A never tiring old friend.

The earliest mention of Kettering in the records is in the reign of Henry I in the 12th century, 1100s, was of a town with approximately 500 population, with a church and a mill and in about 1200, Peterborough under the direction of Henry III gave consent to have a Friday market day.

About this time and up to 1500, new buildings and alterations were carried out on this site.

Other buildings adjoining the church are the Manor House thought at one time to have been occupied by the Sawyer family and before that, was the abbot's hall.

But although the history of the Kettering Parish Church of St Peter & St Paul is generally speaking a little bit vague, especially, regarding the various buildings that were built, pulled down, altered and so on, the present day building, however it came to be, is a magnificent building and viewed from a distance, say from the road from Broughton as you come down the road out of Broughton, is a fine sight, beautifully proportioned, giving a combined impression of strength and beauty in architecture. As good an example of church architecture as any in Northamptonshire.

Fred Blount

October 2000

Fred Blount Memoirs 5

R.F. Blount

Before we leave those early days after the First World War, there are some recollections I have of walking along pavements, eyes on the path and in the gutter, picking up empty cigarette packets and looking inside them, hopeful of finding a card inside. All the children of that era were keen collectors of cigarette cards. All brands of cigarettes would enclose 1 card, 50 to a complete set. Swapping used to go on in the school playgrounds to complete full sets and albums could be obtained to accommodate full sets. Caricatures of footballers, cricketers, boxers, the Cries of London, roses, flowers, wild flowers, actors, motor cycles, cars, to mention a few, and so on.

I had a chocolate box in which I kept my loose cards. This would have been about 1923-1926, and at that time, I had acquired from somewhere, I cannot remember where, a 100,000,000 (one hundred million) mark note and remember being told that a sack full of these notes was completely valueless, such was the state of finances in Germany at that time and, of course, shortly after this, other countries worldwide were much the same, including America. As I remember it, Great Britain survived these bad times as successfully as any country, apart from the very bad unemployment situation. Also, consider the recovery of Germany since those days; today there are about 4 marks to the pound: year 2000. That 100,000,000 mark note would put me in the multi-millionaire category, approximately £25,000,000. It just goes to show the crazy ups and downs of the money market over the years.

In the 1920s we still had the British Empire and no doubt this, at that time, helped us weather the financial storm. How long it is going to last, I do not know, while millions of pounds are being scattered about like confetti among our leading sportsmen, it can only drag down our standard of living in the long term.

Incidentally, the cigarette cards were very colourful, interesting and educational and intended to attract more smokers, but in my opinion, were the only good thing that came out of the packet.

1929/30

At the time I started work in 1929, we used to arrive just before 8 a.m. and assemble in the doorway to our premises until Horace Toseland or Mr Sismey (the secretary, Erny) arrived to let us in. About the same time, a group of smart young ladies used to arrive and assemble in a similar manner on the opposite side of the road and worked for Woodcocks, who had a large ladies' fashion store, millinery, carpets and a funeral department in Victoria Street. We used to eye them up and down prospectively, and pass the time of day across the road. Woodcocks also used to sell curtain materials and dress materials priced up in the windows at such prices as 1/11¾ d per yard (one and eleven pence three-farthings per yard); farthings at this time were still in use as legal tender, being the smallest coin in circulation. The next, the halfpenny, or ha'penny, as it was called, followed by a 1 penny coin, and then the 3 penny bit, the smallest silver coin, or Joey, as it was called, followed by the silver sixpence, or tanner as commonly referred to, and then the silver one shilling piece, or bob, then the 2 shilling piece, or florin, followed by a 2 shilling and sixpence coin, or half-crown, followed with a 5 shilling piece, or 1 crown.

By this time all gold coins had been replaced with paper money: the 10/- note and 1 pound note. Most of this was summed up in a ditty we used to sing:

'Rule Britannia, Britannia rules the waves,
Britons never, never, never shall be slaves.
Rule Britannia, marmalade and jam,
Three links of sausages for our old man.
Rule Britannia, two tanners make a bob
Three make eighteen pence and four two bobs.'

All these coins are now collectors' pieces.

240 pence = £1
12 pence = 1 shilling
24 pence = 2 shillings
30 pence = 2/6 d
60 pence = 5/-
and so on.

There were also £5 notes, £10 notes, £20 notes and so on. Incidentally, going back to Woodcock's young ladies, they were wearing the latest fashion in hats and dress and we, opposite, were wearing the latest in dirty overalls.

Wages were low with the flat rates, or minimum wages, in the shoe trade, engineering and clothing trades for men, round about £2-10 shillings per week, or, if you were on piece work, up to about £4 or £5 per week and in the building trades about 1/4 d per hour: one shilling and fourpence per hour per 44-hour week. By the time I was 22, I was getting 1/7 d per hour.

Between the wars there was a lot of unemployment. My father returned from the 1st World War and when he reported for work at his old factory and job, was given 1 week's work and 1 week's notice to quit. He quickly went round to the Boot Company, later Freeman, Hardy & Willis, who had their own chain of retail shops and obtained a job as a 'clicker' with them, and later a 'sorter' and from then on, never lost a day's work in his life. But most of the numerous factories in the town were on 'short-time', no more Army boots required; the old double-edged sword, the worst war in the history of the world was finished, which was a good thing and a great relief, but with the peace that followed, came a great deal of hardship, unemployment and misery for many years, all over the country and did not really recover until we had gone through another World War.

Fred Blount

October 2000

Fred Blount Memoirs 6

R.F. Blount

My Work as a Plumber and Heating Engineer - Part 3

1936

Messrs Chandler & Newton, contractors from the London area, commenced work on the Bowhill Estate. Mr Chandler himself, from a wooden office on site, organised and managed the site with a site carpenter/foreman.

Quite a number of interesting incidents evolved from the beginning of this site.

First of all, a road was constructed up the middle of the site with kerbs and paths either side, using firstly, large pieces of slag from the local pig iron works or furnaces, of which at that time there was quite a number: Kettering Iron & Steel Co, Cransley Furnaces, Corby Iron & Steel Furnaces, Islip and Irthlingborough Furnaces, any of which could supply broken up slag for roadstone. Then a smaller grade of the same material was spread to form the foundations for a Tarmac road.

The above describes the general procedure for the making of all new roads in this area, except this time things turned out to be not quite normal, as was found out when they came to the procedure of introducing the normal procedure of putting on a heavy road roller, which at that time would be steam powered.

Calamity and dire panic, as the roller sank deeply, with columns of clay rising from between the stones, in blue columns all around the roller. Very quickly, heavy equipment was hired to pull the disappearing roller back on to the main Northampton Road.

Another roller about half the weight and size, but with similar results, and finally a small footpath roller was successfully launched on to that sea of clay.

Looking at the local geology of this site, it shows that all along that valley, there is 200 ft of blue clay in depth, passing under the London Road and the Rugby Ground, which was the site of the old Kettering Brick yard until it was finally pulled down, the chimney and the kiln, in the late 1930s. The pit was used as an infill site for rubbish and eventually acquired by the Kettering Rugby Club, when they moved from the Headlands Playing Fields.

The above paragraph also reminds me of another noteworthy mention of the history of Kettering, the Dust Destructor, a plant which I think was largely subscribed to by the Shoe and Leather Trades of the town. It consisted of a very large steam boiler with a chain grate, fuelled entirely by the town's rubbish, and generating sufficient electricity to power all the town's electric lighting, street lighting, all the numerous factories of the town and also supplying the Co-op clothing with a 6-inch steam main supply for the press room and other uses. This plant also incorporated the tallest chimney in this area and wooden condensers, the water from which was re-used as boiler feed water, and for many years earned us the reputation of being one of the most up-to-date, and forward-looking, and best lit towns in the country and also the cleanest.

This wonderful and remunerative plant served us until it had to be dismantled with the introduction of the Electricity Grid System. It was a great pity that it had to finish, because it solved many of today's serious problems; all the town's rubbish was tipped from the collection vehicles down a concrete chute on to the chain grate of the boiler: bottles, tins and all the refuse. No messing or separating metal and glass. The gases and smoke were released high above the town, no land-fill sites wanted, in fact all that was left in the form of clinker from the boiler was sold and in demand for clinker paths around the district.

I receive a monthly free Heating & Ventilating newspaper, and about two years ago a small column caught my attention headed something like this: "Small USA Town Solves Pollution Problem", and reading it through, it described exactly the same system that we had recently had to close down, after serving for about 100 years. It was undoubtedly the finest investment in the history of Kettering, except perhaps for the Kettering General Hospital, which is another type of story or the Wicksteed Park.

However, getting back to Bowhill, a few months after starting work on the site, Mr Chandler died. He was a quiet, elderly, pleasant man and the foreman carpenter was appointed as site foreman. He was not very popular from then on; I always found him alright. Anyhow, one day he was not being very clever according to today's standards. He was fitting the ground floor joists in the first pair of houses, while one of his arch enemies was topping the chimney and apparently, he said to his mate: 'Watch this, I will get the B-'. He cut a brick in half with his trowel; the other half landed fairly and squarely on the foreman's head. I can see him now running down the site, blood pouring down his face, proving the use of safety helmets.

Early on into the job a labourer was set on, having recently been dismissed from the Co-op Builders. We later were told that the Co-op Building Dept were doing some alterations to the Shoe Dept, in the Co-op Central Stores, where he 'acquired' a pair of shoes only to find out, when he arrived home, that they were not a pair, but both the same foot. Being an enterprising lad, he quickly got over this problem by taking them back that evening to change them. Unfortunately, he was rumbled or recognised and got the sack instead.

About this time, we made a start on the Bowhill Estate, storing all our materials in a lock-up site hut, which included a 7 lb block of Russian fat or tallow, which we used as a flux for wiping soldered joints on lead pipes. This would have been sufficient to have done the pipework to the whole estate of 50 houses. All pipes at that time were lead except for the hot water supplies, which were galvanised iron. However, about three weeks later, I went to get a piece more of the tallow and to my surprise it had all gone. Making enquiries, I was told, 'Oh, yes. Crack had been using it on his boots and also frying bacon and eggs on a shovel over the fire at breakfast and dinner times.' I always said it was one and the same thing as 'Trex', a popular cooking fat at this time. I had to explain to Tommy Capps, my boss at this time, why I required more Russian fat.

Many years later I was employed to put an oil-fired heating system in, at the only detached house on this site - the corner house on Northampton Road, for a Mrs Jackson, previously occupied by Ashbourne, the optician in the town. When this house was built, I did the plumbing to the house, probably the last one to be built and by then we had progressed to using copper tube in place of galvanised iron.

Being a detached house, I think an architect was involved and, as is very often the case, the design of the house could have been better if the plumber was involved at this stage. The kitchen and boiler were at one end of the house and the cylinder and airing cupboard at the opposite end, so that the copper flow and return pipes to the cylinder had to run the whole length of the landing under the boards to the cylinder. As we were putting radiators and heating pipes in, these pipes were exposed and, to my surprise, both pipes had been nailed right through and had never leaked. This took my memory back to the foreman carpenter when he was floor 'bumping', one hit to stand the nail and 'bang' and it was right home; the accurate rhythm of the nail and hammer used to fascinate me, every nail with perfect accuracy and here, before my eyes, was evidence of that skill and accuracy. He should not have nailed my pipes, but at least he did it with such perfection that, for fifteen years or so, they had not leaked, either at the top entry or underneath. The other interesting thing about this was that the nails had completely disappeared due to electrolytic action between the copper tube and the steel nails, leaving only a sharp rusting spike of corrosion that was still holding water.

We have learned a lot about the rights and wrongs of mixing metals in heating and hot water systems since those early days, starting with cheap light-gauge copper cylinders, cheaper than the galvanised iron cylinders used at the time. For a time, we continued to use galvanised iron pipes to the new copper cylinders. The first sign of trouble was in Wallis Road, Kettering, where a leaking connection occurred to a cylinder we had fitted about one year previously. Fortunately, I decided to empty the system down first, and I was then adjusting my Stillsons on to a union connection and the whole return pipe parted from the cylinder, leaving a collection of carbon corrosion in the cylinder, where previously had been a galvanised iron connection. My first experience of Electrolytic Action in water containing oxygen.

Shortly after I commenced my own business, I was doing quite a lot of maintenance work for a foundry and engineering works, Smith & Grace of Thrapston. It was an old-established business, specialising in all sorts of wheels for industry, hydro-electric plant and pulley wheels, that went all over the world; I suppose that they were probably producing munitions through both world wars, as was every engineering works at that time.

However, we were eventually asked to replace the heating boiler as it was leaking and at the end of its life. We took the details: it was a Messenger Boiler from Loughborough. This firm is quite famous for horticultural boilers, mainly for greenhouses, etc. We ordered the boiler, which was subsequently delivered to site, after which we commenced dismantling the old boiler, but there was one thing that bothered me about this operation, that being the chimney which consisted of 2 x 12ft sections about 10 inches diameter, with a heavy bolted flange securing the two sections together, and probably weighing something in excess of 1 ton, probably being cast in their own foundry. How were we going to get this down without risking life and limb? We had not at this stage got round to hiring cranes, so I first inspected the smoke nozzle on the back of the boiler, which scared me further, as all four bolt holes had cracked and it was difficult to see what was holding up the ton of old iron. I quickly made a decision, fetched two long tow ropes and tied them together and tied one end to the bottom of the flue pipe, and laid the rope out towards the open door of the loading bay. I said to my assistant 'When I say "Go", pull like hell and run like hell.' So, the deed was done, it all came down with a terrific crash, chasing us right out on to the loading bay. Not very scientific, but effective and no-one was hurt.

When we were assembling the new boiler, further problems were experienced. Several sections went together, no problems, then one of the top nipples seemed to be unusually tight, but I persevered until suddenly, there was a loud crack and I found we had cracked the section. By this time, I had assembled lots of sectional boilers so I was sure something was wrong. I took the faulty nipple and another one and went and found Jack Smith, who was one of the directors and manager of the Stores and Deliveries, and asked him if he could check the sizes with their equipment. This he did and found the offending nipple to be several thousandths of an inch oversize. We sent the section and the nipple back and received a free replacement and apology.

A Mr Gaylor was the finance manager of the company and early on, asked me to repair his w.c. - a small job, only taking about half-an-hour, so when he asked me 'How much?' I said to him, not to bother, I could lose it in the work at the factory. At this suggestion, he became very annoyed and insisted on a detailed and separate bill addressed to his house. But I survived that experience and did other jobs for him after that. One such job was the repair of a ball valve in the tank in the roof, which I carried out as requested, but when doing jobs in the roof, I always made a practice of inspecting the plumbing generally as people rarely go into the roof. On inspecting the bottom of the tank, I could see a large scab of rust, but no sign of leakage. So before leaving the house, I said to Mrs Gaylor 'You must replace the tank as soon as possible' and then returned to Kettering. This was in the morning and about 4 p.m. of the same day the phone rang. It was Mrs Gaylor to say they were flooded out. I returned with all speed taking a new replacement tank with me. The bottom of the tank had fallen out, leaving a 9-inch diameter hole in the tank. It made quite a mess. I did not expect it to fail quite as quickly as that.

Thrapston at this time had its own gas-from-coal company for the town's gas cooking and lighting, as many of the towns in Northamptonshire did, with their distinctive gasholders nearby. A by-product of these gas works was coke, which was suitable for solid fuel boilers. This was about 1950 and lots of things were in short supply and coke was one of these. I had recently installed a gravity hot water and heating system from a Crane Carlton solid fuel boiler in my house in Roundhill Road, so each night before leaving Thrapston, we called in the gas works opposite Smith & Grace's factory and filled the back of the van with coke and so built up our stock of fuel.

About this same time, an old customer of Tommy Capps moved into a house in London Road, close to where I lived. He used to live in a quiet part of the town, and we were replacing some cast iron gutter that had been broken down by a heavy fall of snow. It was about 8.30 a.m. and all was quiet and peaceful. We had just raised the ladder and were busy screwing side rafter irons on to the rafter feet ready to take the new gutter, when Crash, Clatter, Bang. I nearly fell off the ladder. When we had collected ourselves, we learned that the son of the house was a budding jazz drummer, who had a complete set of drums in his bedroom, and was in the habit of jumping out of bed and attacking his drums, cymbals, etc. first thing in the morning. This chap was later a drummer and percussionist in one of the BBC orchestras.

When later they moved to London Road, one Saturday afternoon there was a knock on the door. It was my old friend and acquaintance, who I had lost sight of. 'Could I do a little job for him?' I agreed and followed him to his house. I removed a gas-fired space heater from the hall, had to fetch a ¼-inch plug from the yard, and then he asked me to repair a cistern and small cast-iron pump on the sink, which was worn out and beyond repair. He then asked me how much. I had known him for a long while, he was deaf and had a habit of trying to turn this to his advantage. I said half-a-crown (two shillings and sixpence, old currency) and he said 'You're joking'; so to avoid any possible mistake I shook my head and he replied with a grin on his face 'I thought you were' and he gave me sixpence. At that I gave up and returned home. I had not reached the kitchen when the doorbell rang and my deaf friend on the doorstep said to me, 'My wife said I did not give you enough.' So, he gave me another six pence and that is how I made my fortune at plumbing (two tanners make a bob).

This chap used the same garage as I did for his repairs and when visiting a factory nearby, remembered he had a letter to post at the garage, no doubt paying his bill. But later he remembered that he had stamped the envelope, so he returned the next day to collect his stamp! He was generally very tight, but a likeable old boy always with a smile on his face, especially, if he thought he had got the better of you. His wife also was very pleasant. I certainly had many more difficult customers to deal with later, some, not many fortunately, who had no intention of paying their accounts and one who, shortly after my association with him, owed me a little over £1700. One meets all sorts in the course of a lifetime of business.

<u>1928/29</u>

>Happy days are here again,
>
>Bright skies above are clear again,
>
>Let us sing a song of cheer again,
>
>Happy days are here again.

The depths of the worst depression in the history of the modern world. So, the songwriters did their best to cheer us up, in between their jazz sessions at this time, with songs as above and the Stein Song, which was another popular hit on everyone's lips at that time; the young ones were easily cheered up, but the elders of the community with responsibilities were not so easily consoled. The multi-millionaires of America, a large number of whom solved their financial problems by throwing themselves off the tallest skyscrapers and ending their worries, and, nearer to home, the political cauldron was beginning to bubble away again. Sir Oswald Mosley with his fascist leanings, the mad painter in Germany with his swastika, Mussolini in Italy, Franco in Spain and so on. I think the best of that bunch was Franco, who did a good job for Spain.

About that time our St Mary's Church Scout Group joined forces with Brigstock & Stanion Scout Groups and camped at Hinchingbrooke Park, Huntingdon. Lord Hinchingbrooke lived in the castle within the grounds at this time. A Mr Tester of Stanion was Scoutmaster at this time and I remember two of their troop were George and Mons Spencer, whose parents ran the timber yard in Brigstock. They had brought their axes with them and went into a spinney on the estate, and a crowd of us followed; they did the felling and we did the dragging out and soon formed an enormous camp fire for the Thursday evening, which was also attended by a group of Girl Guides from an adjoining camp site. I do not know what the estate forester had to say regarding this episode, but we did not go there again. The castle and park are now the property of Huntingdon Council with the General Hospital and an Industrial Site within the walls.

Properties such as this were sold off very cheaply just after the war 1945-1960. In my experience, old rectories with parkland, walled gardens with gardener's cottage for as little as £1700 (Thorpe Malsor) and later Titchmarsh, £7000 in 1960. We did some plumbing and heating on this property, and when I went in preparation to do my estimating I was amazed at the sight of a Lebanese cedar, so much so, that I momentarily forgot the purpose of my visit and fetched a 60 ft tape from my car and measured the girth of the tree at about 4 to 5 ft above ground level: 41 ft and as near as I could get it, approx. 13 ft diameter through the trunk. Shortly after this I visited my son David, who is a keen forester, having served his early years with the Duke of Buccleuch and Boughton Estates. On relating this story to him, we looked through one of his books on recorded specimens in the British Isles, and the nearest we found was a specimen about 9 ft odd (?) diameter through the trunk. At that time, one of the lower branches rested on the floor and no doubt was a nuisance when cutting the grass, so it was cut off and disposed of. After this, we lost sight of the tree and forgot about it until the great storm of 1987 and the second storm 2 or 3 years later and, making enquiries, I was told a strange story. The property had changed hands and the new owner, like myself, was greatly impressed by the stature of this fine specimen and after the first 'blow' in 1987, which the tree quite happily survived, he became alarmed for its safety and had it braced. Then we had the second 'blow' and down it came, uprooted. It is easy to be wise after the event, but would it have survived if it had not been braced? We shall never know.

This garden also had a walled garden, which was quite famous for its contents, as was the owner/gardener Canon Lucock, the previous and last occupier of the rectory, quite a famous and well-known horticulturist. There was at the time we worked on the place, an old, large and very beautiful white wisteria, beautifully scented and up to 3 ft long panicles of bloom on the wall of the house. Also, it was here that I first saw a fine specimen of Romneyer Coultera, with its huge white tissue-paper like, highly scented blooms which ever since, I have been trying to get established in my garden.

At this time, 1960, I had just purchased and moved into my house in Paradise Lane, and could quite comfortably have managed another £3500 on top of the £3500 I paid for Paradise Lane. Business was good and moving forward well. But that is all wishful thinking; I would have liked to have owned that garden, but would I have had the time and the energy to have looked after it? We were always very happy and successful in Paradise Lane, so probably everything was for the best.

I understand all the village had part of the tree for firewood. Certainly, there would be plenty to go round. But it was such a shame that such a magnificent specimen came to its end as it did.

However, back to 1929, the Easter of 1929, I started my working life as a plumber's mate. Today I was reminded of this time, when we cycled to Sywell Aerodrome to see Jim Mollison and Amy Johnson, who were visiting Sywell. Today, Wednesday the 5th of July 2000, I was with Dave and Anne in Brittany, my eldest son and his wife, on holiday. We were at a crossroads watching the Tour de France. Before the event proper comes by, about 2 hours of advertising vehicles precede the race, throwing advertising materials and presents to the crowds lining the route. Among these were a number of Michelin vehicles, from which I acquired a free peaked cap with the Michelin logo on it.

Previous to this, the last time I had a throw-away gift from Michelin was at Sywell in 1929, when they were dropping Michelin Man cigarette lighters from a plane and I managed to get one of these. Amy had just completed her flight from Australia to England. I was 14 years old then. and I am now 85 years old. She eventually disappeared about 1941-42, when ferrying replacement aircraft to France during the Second World War, or it could have been to the Middle East, not France. The Germans had by this time overrun all Europe and a large part of the Middle East. Certainly, we stopped their gallop to victory, but we were lucky. One man, in my opinion, did as much in rescuing us from a desperate situation in 1938, and that was Chamberlain. He met Hitler and signed a treaty and, as the photographs record, came back waving a piece of paper, a treaty which he called 'peace in our time' and twelve months later, Hitler went through Europe 'like a dose of salts' as the saying goes. But Chamberlain had given us twelve long months of feverish effort to recover from the ridiculous disarmament programme that we had been operating since about 1935, burying our heads in the sand and ignoring all the many warnings.

Churchill then came along and took over, and no doubt did a very good job, and saved our bacon. But I still say that Chamberlain gave us that bit of time to recover. He did not get any thanks or credit for this, but he was not quite the 'Old Fool' that the 'Mad Painter' took him to be or this nation's people at that time. They were desperate times, but who knows, those twelve months probably tipped the balance.

<u>1941</u>

On February 15th 1941, Nora and I were married at St Mary's Church, Kettering and about six months later, I carelessly hit a bus with a Series E Morris 8 and three days later woke up in Kettering General Hospital, a bit the worse for wear and eight months later, left the hospital to recuperate and finally went back to work 53 weeks after the accident. This was a fine start to our married life, but we were lucky inasmuch as Nora was still working as a teacher at St Mary's School. She came to visit me every evening for eight months and kept things going, until I was once again able to start work.

The following years, 1941-45, were a difficult period when we had plenty of food for thought on the futility of war and its consequences. When peace finally came, what was to be done to prevent a repetition of this situation which has now become unthinkable, with the new weapons that had developed by the end of the war, finally the Atom Bomb.

The United Nations was formed and so far, seems to be working, as of recent years we have seen whereby a number of would-be new dictators have been successfully dealt with by a force made up of a multi-national army from the United Nations. Perhaps this is the way forward. We all hope so.

In 1945, November, I commenced my business as a Plumber and Heating Engineer and very quickly became totally committed to this latest venture. I had a good start; it was a very hard winter with lots of hard frost and fine snow, which was getting under the tiles and forming drifts in the roof space. Since this time, the Building Regulations have been altered to include a complete covering of reinforced felt, before the slate lath and tiles are fitted.

However, I was kept pretty busy during the winter of 1945-46, removing snow from roof spaces and repairing burst pipes.

Fred Blount

October 2000

Fred Blount Memoirs 7

R.F. Blount
Year 2000

> O dear, what can the matter be,
> Fred's got himself locked in the lavatory,
> Likely to be there from Thursday to Saturday
> Unless Andy comes back with the keys.

Fame at last, I have got my picture in the paper. But what one has to do to achieve this!

After my wife died, it was the end of life as I had known it, after 48 years of a very busy and happy marriage, and a total of 56 years together, including our courting years. I was not doing very well until some of my friends took me in hand and introduced me to the Bowling fraternity. It quickly got me back into circulation again. I joined the Conservative Club Bowling Club and The Lodge Indoor Bowling Club in the winter, and found myself among a new circle of friends. It just about saved my sanity at this difficult time. My bowling friends and my family got me cracking again.

And so, I found myself playing on Thursday evening, on the 8th June 2000 at 6.30 p.m. start at the Pleasure Park against the Midland Band Club. We had quite a good game, but towards the end of the game I was feeling tired (16 ends usually on an evening and 21 ends on Saturday - can be 23 ends with trial ends) so when I saw my friend Fred Elwers, who is the Saturday Captain, I said could he please find someone to take my place on Saturday. Shortly after this, the game finished and we all went into the changing room. After this, we were all going across to the Midland Band Club for refreshment. I was about to leave when my friend Andy Cooper saw me struggling with my bowls bag and said 'Leave it by the door and I will take it to the club.' So, I set my bag down and then remembered that I had not washed my hands and some rather toxic weed killers are used on the greens, so I went back and washed my hands. It took me some time as the paper towels had run out and I had to look around and finally dried my hands on some toilet paper.

When I tried to get out, I was locked in. The door was heavily bolted and barred, the windows were new double-glazed units with security locks. No-one in sight as all the gates are locked to keep out the vandals.

So, I thought, well, they will eventually miss me, but in the meantime, I thought if they do not turn up, I could signal SOS on the light switch when it was dark. But eventually, I could see Andy in the gloom coming to let me out. I joined the others in the club who had carefully saved me some refreshments. They pulled my leg a bit, but it was all good fun. Someone asked me if I had panicked to which I quickly replied, 'You must be joking, what, after spending over 50 years building up and running a business. I knew you would miss me eventually,' which they did, but to be honest, I was relieved when Andy came and let me out. Only this morning, Friday July 21st, I met an old friend who I first met when I was 4, our first day at school and we talked about getting locked in the loo and so it goes on, but it was a bit of fun while it lasted.

All bowlers, wherever we go, have been a great help, and always ready to carry my bowls bag and whilst every bowler takes every game seriously, nobody ever gets upset or criticises your game, if you are off form or old or just not very good, but always you get encouragement. It is a great game and always in the very best company and circle of friends.

1928-29

Bowls is the latest and probably will be my last efforts at sport. From an early age, I was always interested in all forms of sport; my schooldays were taken up with athletics, running, football, rugby and cricket. At the age of 13-14 at Stamford Road School, we had a very good rugby team for our age group under the careful eye of Mr Mole, who was 1st assistant to the headmaster and a very stern but very capable teacher, as were all the other teachers of the school at that time.

Mr House, Headmaster, Mr Mole, Mr Capp, Mr Lilley, Miss Middleton, Miss Barnwell, all well remembered and respected. Matches were arranged on Saturdays. I have vivid memories of playing Burton Latimer at rugby on a pitch at Burton, Station Road (where now there is a row of council houses) with a farm track across the middle of it with ruts and mud about 12 inches deep and after the match, we ran down to the village hall in Church Street, somewhere opposite the church, where there was an old cast-iron 5 ft 6 in bath full of hot water. The idea was to get there as quickly as possible, because there was only one lot of hot water. Thirty of us plastered in mud. I did pretty well; as a good runner I got into the water early on. This was about November 1928, and we won 80 points to nil. About February 1929, a replay was arranged, but the facilities were much better as we played on the Kettering Town Rugby Ground, in the Headlands at that time, with a spectators' stand, all very upmarket and after the match, we ran along to the Royal Hotel, where there was a series of stables or garages. In the stable next to the kitchens, was a large galvanised tank about 10 ft by 10 ft by 2 ft deep with two ¾-inch rubber hoses, one delivering hot water and the other cold water. Much more hygienic than the Burton Latimer facilities, but it was a bit of a shock when someone put the hot water hose on to you, followed by the cold water.

This was the same time as when the Wicksteed Lake was frozen solid: 6 weeks of hard frost, no snow, water 'like a stone', and so was the pitch: no inspection of the pitch in those days. We would have been disappointed if there had been any talk of cancellation anyway, but I do remember I was tackled and brought down; I hit my head on a molehill and cut my eye. On this occasion, Burton Latimer were allowed to play a few old boys, up to about 17 years of age, to balance things up a bit, but we still beat them about 40 to nil.

This old sports ground was on the site now occupied by the Fire Station and Bishop Stopford School and playing field.

After this, I left school at the age of 14 and did not get back into rugby football, but continued my athletics by joining the Congregational Gymnastics Class with other lads of my age: Fred and Andy Grundy, Roy Sinclair, Cyril Underwood, Harry Garret, Arthur Brown and others, whose names are now lost in time, but we all enjoyed this healthy occupation and cannot help reflecting on how lucky we were as compared with the youth of today, who get their kicks from drugs and the like.

At this same time, I was still attending St Mary's Church, having left the choir when my voice broke, but continuing as a server and also as a member of the Bible Class, which held a meeting in the Parish Hall in Lawson Street; they also had a good cricket team and played in the town league.

The Bible Class and cricket team were both headed by Ted Goode. Other Bible Class members were Harry and Len Coe, Herbert Hayes, Harold Townsend and others.

Again, at this time, I was making further progress with swimming and myself and Len Palmer joined the Kettering Swimming Club and Polo team and became quite proficient in diving, having been taken in hand and encouraged by Ginger Turner. Other keen members of the water polo team were Ken Tingle, Ken Brickstock, Harold White and others.

Activities at this time were night school, woodwork, with Frank Arber and Owen Mason as teachers, but none of these evening classes were of any practical benefit to me in my profession as a plumber, and when at the age of 18 I met my wife-to-be, I began to think more seriously of the future and found that in 1933, there were no technical classes available anywhere in Northamptonshire, the nearest being Leicester or Nottingham.

So, in desperation, I started a 4-year International Correspondence Course, which took me 6 years to complete, which without any shadow of doubt was the finest thing that could have happened to me at this stage. I became intensely interested in the theory of my work, while at the same time, I was doing a 44-hour week on the practical side of plumbing and heating.

1934-40

From 1934-40, my spare time was largely taken up with study of my work and about 1940, Wellingborough Tech. eventually started evening classes including plumbing and welding. I joined the evening classes for welding, hoping to pick up the skills of lead-burning. The teacher at that time was a very good welder: oxy-acetylene and arc welding and when I asked him if he could instruct me in lead-burning, admitted that he knew nothing about it, but did the next best thing by getting in touch with the British Oxygen Company and obtained some slides which gave step-by-step instructions on the techniques. From these slides, I quickly became proficient in lead-burning and also welding as applied to plumbing and heating.

On the 15th February 1941, Nora and I were married and on August 17th, approximately six months later, I hit a bus with my Series E Morris 8 and woke up in Kettering General Hospital three days later, left the hospital eight months later, and started work again 53 weeks after the accident. Not very clever and not a very good start to our married life.

St Mary's Church 1920-45

Some of my earliest memories are of being taken to church on Sunday mornings by one or other of my six maiden aunts; later, I joined the Sunday School. Father Glaister was the priest at this time, always wearing a biretta, along with all other very high church practices. He was a quiet and very highly-respected man.

I joined the choir when I was 7-8 years of age. All the choir and servers used to attend a 6 a.m. service on Candlemas day in early February, after which we all walked along to the St Mary's School, if the weather was good. Trestle tables and chairs were set up by Mr Brideman, the school caretaker, and everyone had an enjoyable pork-pie breakfast. Most of the men, choir and servers, worked at one of the local shoe factories and had to be away before 7.30 a.m. in time to clock in at 7.30 a.m. for work. Mrs Crask and other church members would serve at the tables. If the weather was bad, this event was staged in the Cookery Room of the school. I remember Tom Gould, one of the young servers, encouraged by others, on one of these breakfasts, dissolving 40 lumps of sugar in one cup of tea. All the younger members were not in any hurry as we had to get to school at 9 a.m. Some of them attended St Mary's School and so were in good time anyway.

Another annual event was the Sunday School tea party. This often consisted of walking down to the railway station with supervising Sunday School teachers, and catching a train to Oakley station. We got off the train at Oakley and walked across the fields to Great Oakley Hall, where the tea party took place along with other events, and then back across the fields to the station and home. Oakley Hall was at that time the home of Sir Arthur de Capel Brooke and still belongs to that family.

This mid-summer tea party went on for many years, using other venues. Much later, about 1932, when I was 16-17 years of age, a similar party was arranged at Rushton. By this time, we had a curate, Father Rokeby, who took a great interest in the youth of the church. He had formed a guild of young people with a cricket team and he also, on this occasion, had arranged a match in the meadow where the tea party was happening. The team was picked from our members and the pitch was selected on the best piece of grass available (not very good). Father Rokeby was on the opposite side to myself and he insisted on using an old bat with a piece missing from it. Eventually, I found myself bowling to Father Rokeby and I was a fast bowler for my age. He took a swipe at one of my deliveries; I do not know if it was the bumping pitch or the piece missing from the bat, but the ball shot up and hit him between the eyes. The next morning, he was delivering his sermon at the 10.30 a.m. service with two black eyes.

The other social annual event that we looked forward to was the choir outing, which also included the younger members of servers. The first of these that I went on was to Hunstanton. I have a sepia photograph of us all paddling in the sea: left-to-right, Phillip Kirk, Horace Ball, Herbert Long, Arthur Clark, Stan Clarke, Harold Steff, Fred Blount, Arthur Clipstone.

<u>1923-24</u> At this time, Sid Loasby was our Organist /Choir Master. I think on this occasion we were taken in an open-topped charabanc.

<u>1924-25</u> The following year, I think, was London Zoo by train.

<u>1925-26</u> Whipsnade Zoo.

<u>1926-27</u> About this time, Sid Loasby moved to the Parish Church as Organist and Choir Master.

<u>1928</u> Harold Steff also moved to the Parish Church Choir. Mrs Hircock took over from Sid Loasby as Organist and Choir Mistress at St Mary's.

On these outings we became a bit unruly and every year we picked on one individual, pinched his school cap and threw it from the train or bus window, and finished up contributing about 6 pence per head to buy him a new cap.

These were happy days. Father Glaister died about 1932, and Father Rokeby continued to run the church until Father Cooper arrived. Father Glaister lived in a house opposite the roundabout at the end of Windmill Avenue, but after he died a new vicarage was purchased on the corner of Avondale Road and Stamford Road, previously occupied and owned by Mr & Mrs Poulton, who had a shoe factory in Stamford Road, opposite 'The Warren' or Edmund Street. Father Cooper moved into this house when he arrived. He also was a good man, quiet and well-respected. His sermons at Evensong, 6 p.m. to ? were really something. Les Kirk was secretary to the editor of the Evening Telegraph and a budding reporter, and used to take down the sermons in shorthand and one evening timed him: 55 minutes. But he used to visit me when I was in Kettering General Hospital and would talk for perhaps up to an hour without once mentioning religion, but would hold your attention. Another notability of the St Mary's community was Miss Yates, who was housekeeper to Father Glaister.

The choirboys after Sunday 6 p.m. Evensong were allowed into the vicarage until 9 p.m. to play with a collection of games or books.

Fr Rokeby continued this custom after Fr Glaister died. He lived with his mother at 73 London Road, opposite Wallis's Garage. He used to play cards with us and taught us various card games such as Pontoon, Newmarket, Bridge, etc., using coloured counters to record our winnings. When we first had this facility, we raided his fruit orchard. He had a large garden and employed a full-time chauffeur/gardener. The garden extended from London Road about 100 yards down St Mary's Road with a double gate at the top, opening into a drive and brick garage. In/Outside the garage was a trained cherry tree, with large shining black/red cherries. That was our first mistake, until someone ate one, only to spit it out and warn the rest of us. They were morello cherries, very bitter and sour.

The gardener did not take kindly to our conduct, so we were restricted to five minutes at 8.55 in the orchard. Well, the idea was good and Fr Rokeby was a good, patient man, but the three walls surrounding the garden were covered with peaches, apricots, Victoria plums, black plums and pears, and we all spoilt our Sunday suits by cramming fruit into our pockets. More trouble from the gardener. But we survived and this arrangement went on for some years.

Another notability was a Miss Howard, a retired elderly lady, who ran the Sunday School for a period about 1920-25.

Miss Tansley was another well-known church worker, who also had a brother who had a Gents' Outfitting shop in Market Street.

Mr & Mrs Shepherdson: Mr Shepherdson was Headmaster at St Mary's School; Mrs Shepherdson was a keen supporter of the Mothers' Union along with my mother-in-law, Mrs Billings.

Bill Simms was a teacher at St Mary's School and also a server at the church, and well-regarded for his work with the school soccer teams.

Later Claud Harvey came to the school as a teacher and formed a St Mary's School Scout Troop. Later, he left and for a short time taught at the Parish Church School on the Horsemarket. After this, he returned to St Mary's School as Headmaster: another good man who never forgot the young people in his past. In fact, many years later, when a proposed road was being argued in Council, and if it went ahead, it would have closed my business, he stood up in the council meeting and said something to the effect, 'I do not mind what happens to the road so long as you do not interfere with my friend Mr Blount or the running of his business.' I had not seen Claud for about 30 years or more. As it happened, it was such a ridiculous idea, probably thought up at county level by someone who did not know Kettering: a by-pass from Northfield Avenue/

Northampton Road terminating at the junction of the A6 and the Wicksteed Park. This on any Bank Holiday, with the park traffic too, was quite ridiculous and never started. I said from the outset that it would never be done, and a strange thing, although my yard was in the way, nobody ever interviewed me and yet, everyone on the route was interviewed, properties bought, meetings held. I was too small and insignificant to bother with. But I never lost one minute's sleep on the issue and, of course, it all turned out just as I expected! But my old scout friend did not forget me after 30-odd years.

Claud Harvey followed 'Gaf' Potter, or was it Ginger Loake? But Pat Partridge was the last Headmaster of the old Parish Church School on the Horsemarket, and when the new Bishop Stopford School was completed, Pat became its first Headmaster, where he spent the rest of his working life up to his retirement, and also earned himself distinction as the head of probably the best secondary modern school in the town. After Pat retired, Dr Hopkins was appointed as the new head.

All the properties on the railway side of The Crescent were bought by the Highway people. There was to be an underpass under Station Road, continuing along the Crescent and a flyover in the Headlands and continuing up The Close, buying properties in the Headlands and The Close and property at the junction with Pytchley Road. One of my regular customers, Mr E.V. Wright, like many others, was upset because the Headlands flyover would have been close to his front bay window, and he formed an objection committee in objection to the road. All these people's lives upset, and goodness knows how much money spent for what can only be described as a crazy project, which was never started, as I said it would not, when I was first told of it. What a mess! I am pleased I stuck to Plumbing & Heating and avoided the political scene.

Another interesting occasion associated with the old Parish Church School was when Claud Harvey arranged a scout meeting in the hall of the school and Larry Gains, at that time the World Heavyweight Boxing Champion, attended and gave some tips and instructions on the art of boxing. Claud Harvey and his family came from Desborough, and Larry Gains also came from Desborough or Market Harborough. The Evening Telegraph were present and took some photographs and I have a photo-copy of this, showing present Larry Gains, a very tall, very fit and athletic, good-looking chap. The rest left-to-right: 1. Claud Harvey, 2.

Obid Bye (who was St Mary's Church Troop Scout Master), 3. C. Yeomans, 4. ? Giffard, 5. Nick Baker, 6. Frank Pulford, 7. Frank Evans (shown sparring with Ron Bland), 8. Les Clark, 9. D. Stone, 10. Harry Garlick, 11. Larry Gains, 12. Ron Bland, 13. N. Brains, 14. Chuff Hancock,15. Ron Groves, 16. Headmaster, Mr 'Gaf' Potter, 17. ?, 18. ?, 19. Bill Brooks, 20. ?

I was not on this group as at this time this group was the newly-formed Parish Church Scout Troop, later St Mary's School Troop and at this time I was attached to St Mary's Church Troop. Later, when the Church Troop faded out, we joined forces with the School Troop and attended their annual camps with them and came to know Claud Harvey very well.

After this, he eventually took the post as Headmaster of St Mary's School and kept this appointment for several years, finally giving it up and leaving the town to take up work with the Teachers' Trade Union or the T.P.S., Teachers' Provident Society(?). Eventually, on his retirement, he came back to Kettering and lived in Barton Seagrave, and became the Council representative for the Barton Seagrave Ward.

Up to two years ago (1998), the remaining members of the St Mary's Scouts organised an annual get-together and dinner at the Baker's Arms in Queen Street, and took photographs from the various camps that we attended together and reminisced over old times and happy days.

Fred Blount
October 2000
Fred Blount Memoirs 8

The Plenum System of Heating by R.F. Blount

The Plenum System was another significant advance in warm air heating/ventilating systems, mostly used and designed for medium to large public buildings, and introduced in the late 1800s and early 1900s for schools, churches, cinemas, etc.

In the 1800s to mid-1900s and the taking-off of the industrial revolution, things were changing quickly, health problems were being experienced, smoke from all the house chimneys, factory chimneys, coal fires and boilers all belching out smoke and gases from partly-combusted coal fuels. Tuberculosis was high on the list of our health hazards. Sanatoriums were built, open-air schools, tuberculin-testing of dairy cows, pasteurisation of milk were all introduced in the early 1900s to round about 1960 in an urgent effort to eliminate the T.B. scourge, where whole families were being wiped out by this terrible, highly-infectious disease.

In Northamptonshire, industrial problems within the boot and shoe trade with the hundreds of factories, their boilers and also their leather-dust laden operations had their problems, and early on dust-extraction equipment was introduced to each offending piece of machinery to minimise this problem and so, our local industry was slowly, but surely, putting its house in order. At this same time, Kettering and many other surrounding towns were growing in population, with their red-brick terraced houses to accommodate factory workers: more smoke from partly-combusted coal fires.

In the late 1800s and early 1900's some enlightened politicians tackled the education problem of these new areas of industrial growth and their health problems.

In the early 1900's schools such as Stamford Road Elementary School (my old school from 1919-29), Rockingham Road School, Park Road School, Hawthorn Road School and Spencer Street School were all built with similar specifications, introducing a comparatively new type of combined heating and ventilating system, emphasising the health priority with high classrooms, lots of glass to let in the sun, lots of opening windows, but the most important feature, the introduction of the Plenum System; very obvious when one views any of these schools from the outside, all with their tall towers at the base of which is a large fan, pulling fresh air down the tower and pushing the air through a battery of steam-heated coils and on, under the school through large air ducts which are large enough for a man to walk through. Off these ducts are take-offs to each classroom, delivering warm clean air through a 24-inch by 24-inch register at low level, and taking the foul air at ceiling level back into the duct via another return air register, 24-inch by 24-inch. A steam boiler in the basement near the fan provided low-pressure steam to heat the battery of coils.

These plenum systems for some time were regarded as the answer to our health problems in the schools at this time, except for one thing: they had not catered for the soot in the air at this time, and over the period of 20 to 25 years, the floors of the ducts became ankle-deep in soot and other injurious solids from the atmosphere. So eventually, the plenum system was condemned in its original form and replaced with the good old-fashioned radiator and later, with fan-assisted radiators or finned battery heaters.

Also, the positive pressure inside the classrooms caused by the plenum fan was proved to have a tiring effect on the children.

The plenum system was worked upon and improved, by fitting air washers and filters and continued to be used in concert halls and cinemas.

In the schools, other appliances were being installed in the form of fan-assisted convectors of various forms and designs, advantages and disadvantages. One form being above the blackboard, delivering warm air and return air below the blackboard with the eventual criticism that chalk from the blackboard was being blown over the class.

But over this same period 1940-75, the Clean Air Act had successfully got rid of the carbon and partly-combusted coal from the atmosphere. So, all is not doom and gloom and soot, Manchester and London Smog. We are moving slowly in the direction of basics of good health. But now we have Mad Cow Disease, Swine Fever, Salmonella, Asbestosis and other diseases that in the 1920s-30s we did not know existed. Again, over this same period, with our educational standards, the wireless and television, etc., printed health warnings, and still people smoke, hepatitis, etc. Many of these things injuring our health are self-inflicted.

So, what is all this fuss about education? A-levels, university degrees, students being pressurised to a degree where they commit suicide, with the worry of failing their exams. What for? Where are we going? The more education we get, the more trouble and problems we load on ourselves. One step forward, two steps backward.

As I sit here, the television on, they announce that some clever so-and-so has perfected a new drug that will cure hepatitis, and end one of our modern-day scourges. This is good news for those in the community who have become infected through no fault of their own, but for the others, the majority, who through their own fault and careless way of living are infected, it is not going to help them mend their ways. It is something like the race to perfect atomic energy and finally use it for destruction only.

Is this not a step backwards?

How did I wander into this impossible subject from Plenum Heating and Ventilating Systems and the health of the community? Oh yes, that was it: the improvements and failures of a new form of heating.

We seem to stagger blindly forward from one improvement and failure to another. All part of a lifetime of work, most of which we have enjoyed and found interesting. Lots of our younger people find it necessary to use drugs to find relief from the pressures of life, often with a sad result.

Fred Blount
October 2000
Fred Blount Memoirs 9

The Wicksteed Park
by R.F. Blount

One of my earliest memories was about 1919, and being taken to the Wicksteed Park by my parents and some visiting friends from Brighton, to see the beginning of the new lake in the park. Trenches were being dug to start the excavation. I was too young to take in technicalities at that time; it was much later, when I eventually started work, that I became interested in water.

It must have been an interesting venture for Charles Wicksteed, because in his younger days he had operated a business travelling round the rural areas and farms carrying out deep steam ploughing and dredging lakes by the use of two steam engines, one at each end of a field with large steam-powered drums on the underside of each engine, with a long steel cable to which was attached plough shares and by the combined operators of the two engines, the shares were pulled backwards and forwards effectively, deep ploughing large tracts of land, or dredging lakes. This piece of land, with the River Ise running through it, must have presented great prospects of development through his eyes.

The story goes that on his travels and passing through Kettering, he stopped on the bridge over the River Ise to take water for his engines from the river and Lady Hood came by on her horse and said to Charles, 'What are you doing, my man?' to which Charles replied, 'Taking water for my engines, Ma'am.'

She replied, 'That is my water and you cannot have it.'

At this Charles became annoyed and said, 'I will buy this b--- place over your head one day.'

Lord & Lady Hood were the owners at that time of Barton Hall, probably having connections with the famous battleship *Hood*.

As I have said in my earlier pages, these big country houses were selling at low prices, so when Barton Hall and estate came up for sale, Charles Wicksteed was able to carry out his earlier threat and purchased the beginnings of the Wicksteed Park; by this time, he had acquired an engineering works and factory in Digby Street, Kettering.

I suppose during the First World War, it was a munitions factory, but after the War started to make park amusements and park seats.

My earliest recollection of the Wicksteed Park playground was the simple see-saw constructed by a long and substantial plank of wood, balanced and fixed on a fulcrum, and from this primitive beginning other playground products of the factory appeared and were erected for the youth of Kettering to do their very utmost to wreck, but they were so substantially made and erected, that they defied all attempts to damage. The early tippers would be taken 'over the top, 360°' so brakes were fitted to prevent this, but this was probably worse, as they still tried to take them over the top and succeeded in getting them stuck in an upside-down position with brakes jammed, leaving a dangerous job for park staff to deal with. Much the same treatment was given to the jazzes. Then there were slides, swings and roundabouts, rocking horses and park seats: all were tested freely, and without restrictions in the park. At one time, there was a set of rings, similar to those used today in gymnastics. All these things free for the use of Kettering youth. Charles Wicksteed knew that if these playthings could survive the ill-treatment of Kettering's talent, he could safely sell them and send them to all parts of the world, which he eventually did and Kettering became famous for its park and amusements and the factory was kept busy for many years.

Unfortunately, as the fortunes of Wicksteed's factory progressed, all the shoe and leather trades went downhill, suffering from post-war recession; also the clothing trades in the town.

In the 1920s reminiscences of France were cropping up in the entertainment world. Pierrot groups were being formed by amateur entertainer groups, consisting always of a good pianist and a group of good singers, all in the traditional Pierrot costume of loose, baggy trousers and a long blouse with three large buttons down the front. One such group was formed in Kettering; the pianist was Ken Arber, who lived at the corner of Roundhill Road and London Road, and also worked for Charles Wicksteed in the factory office. The leading singer was Frank Evans, a Gents' Hairdresser on Mill Road, Kettering and sundry other entertainers, some children, all in matching costume and suddenly, I do not know how it came about, but they were presented with a wooden structure, well-made, consisting of a stage on the front with steps at each end and changing rooms at the back. Park seats were supplied for the audience, and at some stage I think a collection was made. I don't suppose they obtained very much in the collection box, but it was all good clean entertainment and I think Charles Wicksteed was again responsible for the stage, etc. It was first erected somewhere just behind the cinema or the ice cream factory, as it is now, and after the Pierrot craze faded, it was moved and re-used as a Golf House to the first golf course, which reached from Paradise Lane down to the lake. Later, it was again used by the Kettering Town Harriers as changing rooms. So, it served a good purpose for many interests for many years. But sadly, it finally fell victim to the modern youth of today, who, after several unsuccessful attempts to set fire to it, finally succeeded.

I woke up in the middle of the night, and when I opened my eyes, I was alarmed to see flames leaping into the sky about 20 ft high. My front bedroom looks over the Park, and down to the lake, and over to the canteen on the left. I immediately rang 999, the answer came 'Police, Fire or Ambulance?' I replied 'Fire' and immediately the fire station was on the line and in approximately two minutes, two engines arrived and very quickly put out the flames. But by this time, I could see that it was fortunately not the canteen building, but the old Pierrot building. After that, the remains were carted away and the site tidied up. This was quite recently, 1998/99.

In the early days of the Park, before the canteen was built, there used to be a two-storey cottage or house at the top end of the Park, just below the tennis courts and this at that time was used as a tea room and probably as a tennis club. This eventually disappeared and the new canteen was built.

Many annual events and parties were held in the Park, mostly for Kettering people. The Co-op used to organise an annual tea party for its members and their children. Many cups of tea and bags of sandwiches and cakes - a happy time was had by all. Barton Hall gardens were occasionally opened at this time, and it became quite a common thing for people to visit and pick snowdrops in Lady Hood's spinney.

Kettering at this time finished at the top of Durban Road, with a field gate into the allotments and a path down to the old mill farm. There was an open brook along Water Street, Linden Avenue and Wallis Road, all of which has now been culverted.

The Rowing Club had housing for their boats along the far side of the lake and soon became a well-known rowing club, organising regattas and, with the support of the Park, eventually organised an annual regatta, with the usual boat races against other local clubs. Coloured jars, each with a candle in, lined the bank about 6 ft apart, all the way round the bank. Sports were arranged, and the whole town became involved with this annual event, always finishing with a magnificent firework display. On these occasions the Park was crowded, and no doubt made some money on such days. But quite obviously, also spent lots of money to ensure a successful day. Most things were free those days. Refreshments were sold at the canteen: jugs of tea, sandwiches and cakes.

Rowing boats could be hired at about 6 pence per hour, also punts and canoes, and small motor-boats for four people.

About 1925, work was commenced on the 'New Road' as it was first called and later became Windmill Avenue. St Mary's

Road followed soon after, and access to the Park became much easier.

In the hard winters of the 1920s, the lake often was frozen over and skating enthusiasts used to make good use of it. February 1929 was the hardest and most prolonged frost of the 20th century. It started freezing towards the end of January and for a solid six weeks kept on freezing. The lake was solid ice. People had cars on the ice, bonfires were lit on the ice, and I started my career as a plumber at the age of fourteen after Easter that year. We were mending burst pipes

1 ft 6 in, deep in the ground. It was clear, crisp frosty weather the whole time, not one flake of snow but 29º of frost were recorded that winter.

I remember Mr Aveling, who at that time was Verger at St Mary's Church, Kettering, and who came from somewhere in the fens and in his youth had become champion of all England speed skating. I remember seeing him skating on the lake in great style.

After I left school at the age of 14 in 1929, I joined the local swimming club, who held their meetings in the swimming baths, at that time in Bath Lane, off Bath Road; they also had a water polo club and some competitive diving. There were a covered-in heated pool and an unheated outdoor pool.

I became quite keen and a fair swimmer and quite good off the top board. Eventually, I started attending the outdoor baths every morning about 7 a.m. before going to work. There was quite a group of us; one or two names I can remember: Henry Billson, Ike Bates, Gunty Newman, Alfie Haigh and lots more, whose names I have forgotten. I have a photograph taken by the Evening Telegraph on Boxing Day 1934, showing us all lined up on the bank and also showing six inches of ice over the whole bath except for two holes, broken for us by Mr White, the Bath's Superintendent at the time: one hole at the 7 ft end and one small hole by the steps for Alfie, and clearly marked Alfie, because Ike

Bates was teaching him to swim, but by this time had not quite managed it, so while we quickly dived in and out, Alfie would walk down the steps one at a time. It used to be painful for us to watch him. However, there is a very much more important issue here.

From early April 1934, we had not had a single spot of rain and the bath's water had not been changed for months. One morning, you would go down and the water would have a black crust all over it, and perhaps the next morning, the water would be crystal clear, the aerobic bacteria having completed its function, and the crust had precipitated to the bottom. This went on for some months. The water could not be changed. Both Cransley and Thorpe Malsor reservoirs were bone dry, and water in the town was rationed. Then with approval from Wicksteed Park, a 6-inch main was run along the gutters of London Road, Windmill Avenue, Avondale Road and eventually to the water tower at Clover Hill, and water was pumped from the lake to save the town from a desperate situation.

Eventually, about the end of March 1935, it started to rain and slowly things came back to normality. Of course, if it had gone on much longer, we could have resorted to the breweries, all of which have very large and very deep wells, and we could have drowned our problems in beer. But once again, Wicksteed Park did a great service to the community.

It has just come to my mind that in 1932, when I was 17 years old, and at the same time, when a group of apprentices tested the Water Chute, we supplied the water to the group of bungalows from an open spring in the spinney close by, and while the whole of Kettering was gasping for water, our simple little spring was bubbling away happily, supplying a small community, completely independent and ignorant of Kettering's failing water supply, to which it was also contributing as it would be finally running into the lake. This spring continued to supply the bungalows until about 1995, when the Water Board found out that the lakeside bungalows did not have a 'proper water supply' (?) and Wicksteed Village Trust were requested to put this to rights. So R.F. Blount was on the scene once again after an absence of over 60 years.

When I was 15-16 years of age, we used to carry out plumbing maintenance and repairs to the Wicksteed factory. In the office at that time, men with engineering knowledge were employed: Tom Atwell, Charlie Robbins, Ken Arber and Mr Newbold, the father of one of my friends at this time, was a foreman in the engineering machine shop. At this time also, W. Burton & Son, Montagu Wallpaper and Paint Company, the son of my boss Billy Burton Senior, used to supply Signal Red and Kettering Green and Battleship Grey undercoat paint to the factory, and also large quantities of sheet zinc for pattern-making. This last item came in 36-inch-wide sheets, rolled up and transported in wooden barrels.

One of the factory's specialities was a small hydraulic saw, which was sold to the navy for use on destroyers and battleships for use in the ships' repair shops.

Once when we were working there, they had just taken delivery of a 36-inch circular saw for cutting up heavy steel sections. It comprised a heavy base which could be adjusted through 180º with the saw and would cut through an 18-inch H-iron section at any angle in two minutes, the very latest in engineering achievement at that time. But the general opinion was that Charles and his associates were looking at it with a view of perhaps improving on it and doing something similar themselves.

We were also visiting Barton Hall in the early days of its becoming an old people's home and I was impressed by the old hot water supply system, which comprised a solid-fuel, coke-fired boiler and hot-water cylinder in the basement and a secondary hot-water storage cylinder at the far end of a first-floor corridor, with a secondary flow and return gravity circulation between the two cylinders, from which was taken short hot-water supply runs to basins and baths en route. With this arrangement almost immediate hot water was obtained, a very good arrangement, especially as it all worked by gravity circulation, before the days of small domestic pumps.

The next exciting development was the cycle track, which was well received and appreciated by the local cycling enthusiasts and quickly became a popular venue of local cycle-racing clubs. Jim Aveling and his brother Bob were regularly involved, two sons of the champion ice skater, previously mentioned. Wicksteed Ice Cream tricycles by now had also made an appearance on Saturdays and Sundays and later on Ice Cream Parlours appeared.

Wicksteed's ice cream had become very popular as it was at this time made as I understand in the traditional way, but using goat's milk from Mrs Neale's goats, down by the cycle track. By this time, the late 1930s, J.C. Neale had given up his builder's business in Station Road and had taken the job of Park Manager. Up to this time, J.C. Neale was one of the leading builders in the town; a Mr Sykes was works manager, who also had a son about my age, Claud Sykes, and the whole family were regular attenders of St Mary's Church, Kettering, as I also was. Previously, he had been carrying out building work in the Park for some years.

The next successful enterprise was the laying of a railway track, starting with a station and platform, just below the gardens and across to the left, round the North end of the lake, along the East bank, round the South bank, passing over the sluice gate and on, along the West bank and then cutting across and back to the station. On this track a Diesel-engined model train pulls a series of trucks, trailers with wheels and platforms, open-sided and with suitable seating. Probably, the most successful of all the Park's introductions, carrying upwards of perhaps 100 visitors per trip, lasting about 15 - 20 minutes for a very reasonable fare and very popular with the visitors. Until this time, this was probably the only park of its kind in the country, but war clouds were gathering, and lots of our pleasures were about to disappear.

In the early 1920s a popular annual event was organised, involving all the Kettering and District schools. It became well-known as the Fineshade Cup, which was a competitive swimming race and in the early days, was competed for in the lake at Fineshade Abbey, but later, for some reason or other unknown to me, the venue was changed to the Wicksteed Park, from the bank somewhere in the vicinity of the model boating pool and across to the big island and back - something in the order of 100 yards. On this annual occasion, Charles Wicksteed was in the habit of inspecting the course from a boat before the race, and on one of these occasions, was in the boat with a friend of mine doing the rowing. Quite suddenly and unexpectedly, Charles says, 'Jump in and see how deep it is.' My friend hesitated, Charles did not, jumped in and satisfied himself as to the depth of the water, waded to the bank, got into his two-seater Humber car, where his canine friend, Jerry, was patiently waiting, drove home and changed into dry clothes. Nothing to it! All in a day's work. My friend, the rower of the boat, was Billy Wells, who at that time worked in the factory and part-time in the Park.

The last summer I was at Stamford Road Schools, 1928 I think, the Stamford Road Schools won this event and, in fact, several previous years. The cup was held for twelve months by the winning team, and I remember Fred Abrahams was our star swimmer at this time. The trophy was quite a good-looking one but I do not know its history, who presented it or how the event came into being.

About 1930, Kettering town achieved Borough status and with it a Building Inspector who had to enforce minimum or standard rules within the building industry. This duty he carried out fairly painlessly. The Wicksteed Park came into his jurisdiction, where Charles Wicksteed had had enjoyment of freedom on his own property, but now had to conform within the town's boundary which finished on this side of the town at the River Ise.

The Wicksteed Park at this time had planned to build a number of bungalows within the Park for their employees. Outside the confines of the Borough, the inspector had no say in the matter and so, the bungalows were eventually built on the Barton Seagrave bank of the Ise, near the water chute, where the by-laws were less stringent at this time.

I was seventeen at this time and was given the work by my boss, W. Burton & Son, of carrying out the plumbing to these bungalows. The water supply was from a spring in the spinney just beyond the bungalows, which gave just enough head of water to supply bath, basin and sink. When I visited these bungalows many years later, I was surprised to find out that in mid-winter how warm and comfortable they were, and the water supply was still supplying their needs until the Water Board requested that mains water was installed, but as I have mentioned elsewhere, in 1934, when the two reservoirs ran dry and Kettering was drinking water from Wicksteed lake, the spring was still running happily.

Fred Blount

October 2000

Fred Blount Memoirs 10

The Headless Chicken
by R.F. Blount

About 1935/36. At this time, I worked for Tommy Capps; we were working at the White Hart, Queen Street, Geddington. The landlord was Billy Halloway and his hobby was rearing and showing Bantams; they were fine-looking birds, very colourful, but unfortunately, a very fine-looking cockerel had a nasty habit of flying up and pecking one's neck when you turned your back on it and unfortunately, Billy let them run free-range in the pub yard. Shortly after commencing work, my mate, a Geddington lad, came into where we were working with a piece of galvanised iron pipe and complained that this bird had just pecked his neck, so I said to him, 'Carry your steel rule in your hand and give it a clout.' We both carried a 2 ft steel rule in a special pocket in our overalls - it was hinged in the middle -12 inches long, opening up to 24 inches.

Shortly after, my mate Bill Moore came in and said, 'I did as you suggested and I have cut its head off, and it is running round the pub yard without a head.' Of course, it did not run for long. Billy Halloway was very annoyed, as it was his prized bird.

I related this story to my children many years later, when my daughter Margaret was at school at the Convent School in Hall Lane, Kettering. Shortly after this, she was taking an English exam on a subject of their own choice. She repeated this story and scored top marks and had to read it out to the whole class. This would be about 1955/60.

At the time I worked for J.T. Capps, it was quite common for hot water systems to become 'air locked'. It was always an indication of bad pipework and bad workmanship. We had two customers where this happened on a regular basis: Barlow's Bakehouse, Stamford Road, Kettering and Mrs Trevor Spence, corner house of St Peter's Avenue and London Road, Kettering. We were used to dealing with these jobs in a similar manner and it always involved two men and 3 ft of ¾-inch rubber hose, connecting the hot and cold supplies over the sink with the rubber hose, turning on the hot-water tap first, and then the cold-water tap, using the town pressure cold water to remove the air lock.

We were called to Mrs Trevor Spence to deal with an air lock. We were always on our best behaviour on these occasions when we worked here. She was a very smart, well-dressed woman, the house was immaculately furnished with wall-to-wall fitted-carpet throughout the house. Anyway, we got to work, listening for the rumble which indicated that the air lock had moved, but no rumble, but I heard splashing noises from somewhere upstairs. Dashing upstairs, I met water coming from the w.c. at the top of the stairs and subsequently, found that someone had fitted a vent pipe over the cistern, no doubt in an effort to cure the air lock. Down the stairs to fetch a bucket and floor cloth, I met Mrs Trevor Spence and said, 'Sorry, we have had an accident, can I have a bucket and cloth,' which she quickly supplied and I started mopping up. I was thinking, I shall get the sack for this, but turning round, there was Mrs T.S. busy mopping up with me. After getting her red carpet as dry as we could, she fetched an electric fire and went out of her way to reassure me that it would dry out and be none the worse for its accidental wash.

After this episode, she always asked for me to do her repairs and when eventually I started my own business, I still did her repairs. By this time, Mr Trevor Spence had died, and she had moved to a house in the Drive, off the Headlands, and later to Bournemouth.

For many years, I took 'The Heating, Ventilating & Air Conditioning Magazine' and I remember a full-page advertisement by Spirax, who manufactured and sold steam equipment including air eliminators and steam traps. The advertisement was a photograph of a gravestone on which was an inscription:

> Where e'er you be,
> Let wind go free
> For it was the wind
> That killeth me.

Further to my remarks on the 'Dust Destructor', as it was generally referred to by the man in the streets of Kettering, when referring to the valuable asset to the town, the rubbish collection, which fuelled the steam boilers and electrical generators, in addition to providing power and light to the town, it also had another well-used facility: sterilising rooms and plant. In the early 1900s, there were frequent epidemics, such as scarlet fever, smallpox, erysipelas, diphtheria and others, when all clothes, bed clothes and house contents were taken to the sterilisation unit and sterilised, and then returned to their owners. Also, at this time in some of the poorer parts of the town, some of the properties had flea and bug infestations; these too were dealt with in a similar manner, plus a visitation by a specialist team from this department to fumigate these houses.

This reminds me of another incident in the adjoining Kettering Electricity Works. I was called to a Mrs Hobbs in Hawthorn Road to repair a burst pipe. The lead pipe water main came into the house just inside the front door, rising to the bathroom above. The front door was North-facing, and the draught from the door was responsible for the freezing and bursting of the pipe which was badly split. I cut the pipe through in preparation to put in a new piece of pipe, and then bent the two free pipe ends away from the wall. The door and pipe were about 10 ft from the bottom of the stairs. The next thing I knew was picking myself up from the bottom of the stairs. I held an insulated screwdriver gingerly to the two ends of the pipes and a 2-inch spark was jumping from one pipe end to the other, with minor explosions.

I went upstairs to the bathroom, where I knew there was an old Densacone electric water heater for the bath. Water was running from the bottom of the heater where all the 400-volt electric supplies were connected; further investigation revealed that the electrician (?) had earthed the appliance to the nearest lead pipe. A very good earth, yes, but the poor unsuspecting plumber who cut the pipe in half, me, collected 400 volts. At this time, in the Plumbing Trade Journal there was a witch hunt in progress about this very same problem, and trying to outlaw this practice, and make the electrical authorities provide their own earths, which eventually came about.

However, I was jumping mad, lucky to be alive and jumping. I made my way hot-foot to the electricity works and met one of the foremen of the department just leaving the office. I nailed him and gave him the length of my tongue and lectured him on the spot on the evils of earthing on to our water pipes, to which he calmly said, 'Why did you not turn off the electricity at the main?' to which I replied, 'What, to mend a burst pipe? I turned off the water and thought that was enough.' I felt sorry for the chap after I had cooled down. I did give him quite an ear bashing. He also said that it should have blown a fuse. Well, it blew my fuse, but I replied, getting a bit fed up with a ridiculous situation, 'Well, you never know, perhaps someone mended the fuse with a 4-inch nail.'

Old Mrs Hobbs had three sons all of whom worked at Clarke & Hobbs, Plumbing and Heating Supplies, Station Road. Joe Hobbs and his wife used to attend the Parish Church of St Peter & Paul. Mrs Hobbs used to be interested in Art and Painting and took quite an interest in the wall paintings in the Nave.

But returning to the Dust Destructor, it was undoubtedly, the most useful and forward-looking possession and plant that Kettering ever possessed, the answer to one of our ongoing problems of our modern world and will be increasingly so, with our ostrich-like stupidity of burying our rubbish in convenient holes in the ground, which just create and emit poisonous gases into the atmosphere. We cannot get rid of our problems by burying them - they are bound to come to the surface in the form of deadly gases.

Whereas all these gases were burnt off, and all that was left was incinerated metals and glass in the form of clinker, which was used by the council or sold to builders for the construction of roads and paths. Nothing was wasted and no harmful residue left to dispose of, and the whole town's energy and lighting and power supplied in the process. When the grid system arrived, this wonderful plant became redundant and was dismantled. A backward step for Kettering and indeed the whole country. If, instead of the grid system of electrical energy, more similar plants were built like Kettering's, it would have solved most of our pollution problems. The principle of the grid system was good up to a point, whereby power stations were built near where the coal pits existed, but our old system was fuelled by the town's rubbish, not coal!!

Since I started my previous passages and earlier remarks regarding the advantages of burning our rubbish via the Kettering Dust Destructor, and the disadvantages of burying our rubbish, ostrich-fashion, out of sight, out of mind, with all its evils, I have picked up a book that I bought, but had not read on this very subject.

Having read it, it illustrates most of what I have said in the previous paragraph, in the old St Austell China Clay pits in Cornwall.

My interest in this project was started 4 or 5 years ago, when I visited 'The Lost Gardens of Heligan', which was an old Cornish garden (one of many Cornish gardens) that for some reason had fallen into decay and neglect, and was rediscovered by Tim Schmit and his friend, John Nelson. They were attracted by colour in the undergrowth and tangle of briars and found it to be a very old and neglected garden, full of collections of plants, by some wealthy landowner and plant collector, probably in the 1800s, when plant collectors such as Robert Fortune, Tom Forest, Frank Kingdon-Ward, etc. in their heyday, were collecting and sending back to their supporters lots of rare and exciting exotic plants. On further investigation, glass houses, pineapple frames and sophisticated heating systems were uncovered. With obviously a lot of hard work and expense, it was eventually opened to the public. Apparently, the property had not been occupied or cared for, for about 70 years, but lots of interest was generated in the horticultural world and it became the largest garden restoration project in Europe. Lots of manufacturers of horticultural equipment and voluntary work showed up, and helped to promote the venture and a lot was learned in the process.

From this same team and enthusiasm came another venture, which also touched upon one of my oldest interests, the environmental problems over water supply, the air we breathe, the manner in which we deal with our household and industrial rubbish by finding and paying for a large hole, and feverishly filling it with our rubbish, like the ostrich burying its head in the sand. As I have said before, we cannot do this and get away with it; all the evils and poisons come to the surface and pollute the atmosphere.

When I was 16 years of age, I was taking two plumbing trade journals: 'The London Plumbing Trade Journal' and 'The Manchester Plumbing Trade Journal' and it was in the Manchester Journal that I read of a young doctor, about 1931, fresh from medical college, who joined a surgery and noticed that a lot of his patients had similar stomach troubles and symptoms, and carrying out tests, found that they all had advanced stages of lead poisoning. This was in the Chester area where the surrounding land was largely heath land and acid. What they did about it I do not know; but about 1975, they banned the use of lead for drinking water supplies and for all new building projects, the specification for plumbing started off with the passage 'remove all lead water supplies and replace with copper, plastic, PVC, etc.' But it will take many years before all underground services will be removed. 2000 years of civilisation to find out that lead was unsuitable for the conveyance of water.

About three years after this, about 1934-35, I was taking a journal, 'The Surveyor', and read an article regarding a modern method of handling sewage where it was collected into a large reservoir, something like a gasometer, where it was heated and methane was driven off and sold. One of these early systems was installed in the British sectors of Bombay and Calcutta. But on the other side of the cities there was very little in the way of sanitation, and it was pretty messy. The article was written to point out that we cannot separate disease quite as easily as this.

Anyhow, the team from the Lost Gardens of Heligan were looking for a suitable site to build a new series of gardens where they could collect and display plants from all parts of the world. They finally found what they wanted in the old worked-out pit where china clay had been dug out for a hundred years.

Early this year, we had been to Brittany on holiday and, coming back, my son David suggested that we called in to look at the new 'Eden' site to which I quickly agreed as I had been watching its progress ever since visiting 'The Lost Gardens'. My immediate reaction on seeing the site was what a wonderful change it was to see such a large hole being made use of in this way, instead of filling it with and burying our rubbish in it, materials no longer of use so bury them, out of sight and out of mind or burying it in the sea: criminal behaviour. Parking was easy and then we queued up to put on our safety helmets and jackets, along with lots of other visitors and parties of school children. I turned to a chap next to me and said I have been in the building trade for over 70 years, but it is the first time I have worn a safety helmet. But I must admit even that was a step in the right direction. The pit is huge in area, they say equal to the area of 35 football pitches.

Work started on the site on October 15th 1998, and although very little capital was available at this stage, lots of capital was put into the scheme as it progressed.

Alfred and Sir Robert McAlpine, who had not worked together since 1972, were jointly awarded the building contract and great progress was being made at the time of our visit, and it was also very impressive using revolutionary methods of building and materials. Having read the handbook for sale in the restaurant and shop on the history and forward planning of this enormous new venture, it gives a welcome feeling of relief and confidence for the future of the environment and education in this direction and also horticulture. I am looking forward with excitement and interest to revisiting this site when work is completed, and the various astonishing buildings and conservatories are filled with specimens from all corners of the globe.

With the pollution problems cropping up in every avenue of our lives, burying our rubbish, exhaust fumes from our various forms of transport and industrial machinery and the ever-increasing problems with water supply quality, the overcrowding of our road systems, even the air is getting overcrowded with air travel, so any effort to tackle these problems is a welcome change, and I feel that the Eden project is a step in the right direction. After all, plant life and forests exchange our polluted atmosphere back to life-giving oxygen, and so nature is constantly trying to correct our stupid headlong rush to more and more pollution.

So, what is the answer to our problems? Certainly, the replanting of some of our old forests should be carried out and help nature to help us. But in the meantime, we seem to be getting ourselves into ever more deeper troubles. About 12 years ago, I gave up taking any daily papers, objecting to the scandalous rubbish and polluted gossip that they use for headlines in every edition of every paper with lurid details to follow. Only this morning, I visited a friend of mine while waiting for my car to be MOT'd and picked up a daily paper, which headlined a new venture by a number of schools for a trial period, with a possible extension to all schools, the free issue every morning to senior girls, of free anti-pregnancy pills without parents' knowledge or permission. What are we coming to? Are we deliberately putting up a fight against nature? If so, I know which one I would put my money on. I have already said that nature has an answer to all our stupidity, and this item is no exception. There have already been deaths from these pills by overdose.

Who is going to pick up the bill when parents sue after such an incident? Who is going to pick up the bill when parents sue for AIDS, because this is sure to follow, with children being encouraged to take part in this free-for-all against nature. It has an answer to our problems, but I do not like the answer in the future to this particular problem. Probably, the worst form of pollution yet? So perhaps, I should start taking newspapers again, at least the general public are warned in advance of some of the things to come and their possible repercussions.

But enough of all this drear and doom. Once before, I was carried away from the subject in hand on to our present-day problems. So back to Eden and hope for the future. I feel that the Eden Project, and the investors, and team behind it have started looking for some of the answers. In any event, the filling in of this huge hole with something far more interesting than our rubbish, is to be applauded and encouraged.

Fred Blount

January 2001

Fred Blount Memoirs 11

Holidays - Solva, St David's, Pembrokeshire 1960 - 1970

by R.F. Blount

In the early 1960s, we found a very good farmhouse at the top of the hill going south from Solva. It was so good that we kept going there for several years. The farm was kept by Mr & Mrs Richards, with whom we struck up a lasting friendship; only this morning, I had a Christmas card from Mrs Richards - her husband died about 1970.

The food was wonderful; we used to joke about the chickens - by the size of the chicken legs we used to say they were ostriches. They were free-range in the farmyard. We had to avoid eating during the day in preparation for the evening meal. The breakfasts were much the same.

In my opinion, the Pembrokeshire coastline is one of the most beautiful pieces of scenery in the British Isles, especially at the end of May, about Whitsuntide, when the coastline and hedges are ablaze with colour and wild flowers, the cliffs and rocks along the beaches covered with wild flowers, as good as any laid-out alpine garden, or maybe better - more realistic - bluebells, primroses, cranesbills, thrift, bladder campion, violets, ragged robin and numerous other members of wild flower families.

Lots of beaches, some of them large and lots of small beaches, only reached by narrow paths down the cliffs, all having their stories and history. Some of them have in the past been thriving communities, with still-existing buildings, evidence of the past, many of them being involved in the transport of quarried roadstone, sometimes the stone being transported overland from the quarry by cable containers on pylons to the beach, and shipment to all parts of the United Kingdom.

One year, about 1968, we awoke to a dull, dreary and very wet morning; beaches were out of the question, so after a good breakfast, we decided to drive south down the Gower peninsula in hopes of finding sunshine. Down through Haverfordwest, and finally hitting the south coast of Pembrokeshire at a small town by the name of Saundersfoot, nice little place but on a wet day as bad as anywhere else without the sun. So, we found a café and had some light refreshment and decided to move on. We returned to the car park which was a large jetty and were about to move off, when an old flat-tank motorbike arrived; its rider was dressed from head to foot in goggles, leathers, boots, coat, helmet and gloves and a large acetylene lamp on the front of the machine. I went over and while I was looking at it, several other motorcycles arrived, all of which were obviously old and very interesting. So, we changed our minds and stayed to see what it was all about. Eventually, there were 53 of them and they set them all up in the rest of the car park and I purchased a programme of the event. It was an annual event, organised by the Vintage Motorcycle Club, and dated Saturday and Sunday 7th & 8th September 1968, being the 13th Annual Gloucester to Saundersfoot Run.

<u>The Route</u>. After leaving Gloucester on Saturday 7th September, the competitors will follow a route along the A40 through Huntley, Ross-on-Wye, Monmouth, Raglan, Abergavenny, Brecon (midday), Senny Bridge, Llandeilo, Carmarthen, Red Roses and Kilgetty, and are expected to arrive at Saundersfoot from 4.00 p.m. onwards.

This was fine, the weather too had improved, it had stopped raining and brightened up, so I fetched out my camera from the car and proceeded to take some photographs of these interesting machines. I am sorry to say that I did not get them all, but I managed about 30 35mm coloured transparencies, and along with the details on the programme, they make very interesting viewing.

'An event of this nature cannot be organised without a great deal of hard work from a lot of people. The Vintage Motorcycle Club wishes to express its thanks to the Saundersfoot Harbour

Commissioners, Messrs Vic Morris Ltd, and Mr and Mrs Parker of the Gower Hotel, and last but not the least to the competitors and spectators without whom there would be no rally.'

The Saundersfoot Run

Now in its 13th year, the Saundersfoot Run has grown into a major event in the calendar of the V.M.C.C. It was the first two-day event to be organised by the club, and from a very small beginning, it now attracts an entry of about 50 and is still growing.

Membership forms and any other information regarding the Vintage Motorcycle Club, may be obtained from the Secretary, Mr E.E. Thompson,

>28 Glover Road,
>
>Pinner,
>
>Middlesex

Entrants

No 1. Johnny Thomas (Nantgaredig). 1904 Humber forecar. This machine has handle starting through a leather cone clutch, all chain drive, two speed gearbox. Has previously competed in the London to Brighton run, and finished within the time limit.

No 2. Jim Wheeler (Hallow). 1912 Triumph, 3½ h.p. 3 speed hub gear. Another of the famous trusty Triumphs, testimony to the numbers which still survive. This one has been in the family since 1920.

No 3. Felix Burke (Cheltenham). 1913 Williamson. The Williamson is a flat twin water cooled machine of 962 c.c. fitted with a two-speed gearbox. The sidecar is a coach built E ramble and is painted in the colours of the 1912 show model. This outfit cost £99 in 1913.

No 4. D. Harris (Cookham). 1913 Triumph, 3½ h.p. Belt drive with a 3 speed Sturmey Archer hub gear.

No 5.   Mrs B. Hallard (Studley). 1914 Rover, 500 c.c. This machine is fitted with an Armstrong hub gear, one of the many available at that time.

No 6.   Dave James (Tenby). 1915 Wolf, 2½ h.p. single speed. Believed to be the only one of its kind in the club.

No 7.   J.C. Hyatt (Reading). 1916 Harley Davidson, 1000 c.c. 3 speed all chain drive. This is an early specimen of one of America's best known motorcycles.

No 8.   J.T. Davies (Hatton). 1919 Triumph Model H, 4 h.p. Chain cum belt. An example of what is perhaps the most famous Triumph ever produced.

No 9.   G. Smith (Cardiff). 1920 Sunbeam, 500 c.c. Side valve, 3 speed all chain drive. This machine is as found. It is the first Saundersfoot for both machine and rider.

No 10.   G.E. Blatchley (Cardiff). 1920 Ivy, 249 c.c. ladies' model. 2 speed all chain drive.

No 11.   T.R. Hopes (Cardiff). 1921 Beardmore Precision, 350 c.c. Sleeve valve, 3 speed all chain drive. This machine is fitted with the famous Barr & Stroud sleeve valve engine.

No 12.   G. Burrow (Ombersley). 1922 Sunbeam, 4¼ h.p. 3 speed all chain model. For the mathematically minded, Mr Burrow was 31 years old when he bought this machine new.

No 13.   Mrs R. Davey (Walton-on-Thames). 1923 Royal Enfield, 225 c.c. all chain drive. Gent's model – Lady driver L. Plates, gas lamps, token brakes obviously trying to outdo the old man.

No 14.   W.C.S. Phelps (Cardiff). 1923 Triumph, 557 c.c. side valve, 3 speed, pulling a Watsonian feather-weight sidecar on its eighth Saundersfoot outing.

No 15.   W. Cox (Weybridge). 1923 Raleigh, 350 c.c. chain-cum-belt. 3 speed model.

No 16. E.W. Forster (Walton-on-Thames). 1924 Sunbeam, 347 c.c. all chain drive 3 speed. This Sunbeam was found in pieces. It is in its 5th successive season and the owner is looking for any catalogues containing pictures of this model.

No 17. G. Hallard (Studley). 1924 A.J.S., 799 c.c. Vee Twin 3 speed all chain drive. This machine has recently been restored, the Coventry to Brighton run being its first outing this year.

No 18. F. Garland (Ammanford). 1925 New Imperial, 2¾ h.p. O.H.V. 3 speed all chain drive. Third Saundersfoot run for this machine.

No 19 G. Gardiner (Barry). 1925 Scott, 600 c.c. 2 speed model. One of the many from the stable of this dedicated Scott owner.

No 20 W.C. Davies (Brynamman). 1925 Triumph, 500 c.c. 3 speed all chain drive.

No 21 R.C. Richens (Claverham). 1926 Douglas E.W. model, 348 c.c. 3 speed all chain drive. The E.W. Douglas was the first mass produced machine from the Douglas works and was very much in advance of its time.

No 22 D. Dagnall (Cheltenham). 1926 A.J.S. Combination, 799 c.c. Vee twin 3 speed all chain model. A very powerful outfit capable of holding its own even today.

No 23 S. Doyle (Coventry). 1926 B.S.A. 496 c.c. side valve three speed – all chain drive. An example of the 'go anywhere' type of motorcycle available in the vintage era.

No 24 R. Ifor-Roberts (West Drayton). 1926 Royal Enfield, 350 c.c. 3 speed.

No 25 D. Cox (Chaddesley Corbett). 1927 Scott, 596 c.c. Another specimen of the famous 2 speed model.

No 26 E.J. Williams (Gwaun-cae-Gurwen). 1928 Sunbeam 500 c.c. This machine was in daily use for thirty years by two miners, carrying them to and from a coal pit, seven miles away from their home. Both men weighed over 16 stone each.

No 27   L. Hurrell (Bishops Cleave). 1930 Brough Superior S.S. 100, 996 c.c. A fine example of perhaps the greatest motorcycle ever made.

No 28   R.J. Kitchen (Cheshunt). 1930 Sunbeam, 493 c.c. 3 speed all chain drive. This machine is fitted with a swallow sidecar.

No 29   A. Mitchell (Solihull). 1930 Scott, 498 c.c. 3 speeds. A regularly ridden machine both as everyday transport and vintage competitor. Takes in almost all local events and a number of long-distance events as well.

No 30   M.G. Griffiths (Malmesbury). 1932 Rudge, 250 c.c. Rudge machines were very popular in the thirties and enjoyed a high reputation as a quality built machine.

No 31   L. Cooper (Newport). 1932 B.S.A., 350 c.c. O.H.V. solo. One of the twin-port sports models in very nice original condition.

No 32   D. Pryke (Birmingham). 1934 Ariel, 600 c.c. O.H.C. four speed all chain drive. A forerunner of the famous Square Four range of machines. Technically, it is with its overhead camshaft, one of the most interesting of the Square Four range.

No 33   P. Ward (Malmesbury). 1936 B.S.A., 499 c.c. O.H.V. Second Saundersfoot for this machine which should prove to be very reliable.

No 34   P.A. Moffat (Gloucester). 1938 Brough Superior, 998 c.c. This machine was exhibited at the 1938 Motor Cycle show. The rider is a past President of the V.M.C.C. and is accompanied by his wife who is the only lady vice president of the club.

No 35   P. Davey (Hersham). 1938 Triumph Model 2H, 248 c.c. The cooking version of the Triumph Tiger 70. This machine had given daily service to its original owner from 1938 to 1967 when it was pensioned off, only to be rescued for the modest sum of £5 by the present owner, and restored for a further £20.

No 36   J.A. Bates (Redditch). 1939 Brough Superior and sidecar, 998 c.c. Brough Superiors seem to be very popular this year.

No 37   H.O. Gurr (Gt Brickhill). 1928 Norton, 490 c.c. Mr Gurr is well known for his impeccable restorations. No doubt this machine will be up to his usual standards.

No 38   H. Whittaker (Evesham). 1914 Triumph, 550 c.c. This machine is fitted with a 3-speed hub gear.

No 39   G.D. Francis (Clevedon). 1915 B.S.A., 4¼ h.p. Single cylinder three speeds Chain cum belt. This machine was restored two years ago and has been a regular competitor in V.M.C.C. events since. It is fitted with a 21 plate clutch, which the owner says, has two positions, in, or out.

No 40   W Evans (Brynamman). 1928 Zenith, 172 c.c. 3 speeds all chain drive. This is the first run for both machine and rider. The machine has a T.T. super sports engine and early electric lights.

No 41   W. Land (Cheltenham). 1929 Scott, 498 c.c. Mr Land is a regular award winner.

No 42   W.J. Flew (Bristol). 1927 A.J.S., 496 c.c. and sidecar. Wally is a regular competitor in the Saundersfoot run.

No 43   G.J. Flew (Bristol). 1929 A.K.D., 150 c.c. 3 speed all chain drive.

No 44   Miss C.J. Flew (Bristol), 350 c.c. 3 speed all chain drive. Once again Carol is riding the same machine which has been so successful in previous V.M.C.C. events.

No 45   M. Thompson (Cardiff). 1926 Scott, 596 c.c. 2 speed. Fitted with long saddle tank. Renovation incomplete so that it can be used in rallies this year.

No 46   F. Ridealgh (Weymouth). 1925 N.U.T., 700 c.c. Vee Twin. Nut, stands for Newcastle-upon-Tyne where the machines were manufactured from 1912 to 1933.

No 47   P. Harris (Codsall). 1920 B.S.A. 3½ h.p. and sidecar.

No 48   A. Thomas (Kilgetty). 1925 Levis, 247 c.c. Model K. A Pembrokeshire rider on his fourth Saundersfoot.

No 49   W. Cooper (Bristol). 1937 Scott, 596 c.c. Another of these famous water-cooled two-strokes.

No 50   M. Jones (Pembroke). 1920 Calthorpe, 2¾ h.p. Two speeds, chain cum belt.

No 51   P. Ward (Malvern). 1911 Edwell, 3½ h.p. The Edwell was manufactured by the late Edmund Williams at Bromyard about 1911. It was fitted with the "Perfect" engine and was thought to be of an advanced design for its time.

No 52   J. Moore (Reading). 1903 Anglian, 247 c.c. Single speed. The sole surviving example of this make.

No 53   J. Hill (Exeter). 1926 Velocette, 249 c.c. Two stroke. This is a model H3 with duplex cradle frame and an engine driven oil pump.

What started out as a dismal disappointing day finished up as a very interesting and happy

experience, after which we returned to the farm to the wonderful meal that was awaiting us.

Fred Blount

December 14th 2000

Fred Blount Memoirs 12

Trebah Gardens, near Falmouth, Cornwall
by R.F. Blount

On one of my recent holidays with Nene College, Northampton, based at a very nice and comfortable hotel on the seafront at Falmouth, we visited the Trebah Gardens.

The owner had us all assembled in front of his house at the top of a beautiful valley running down to the sea and he then gave us an interesting introductory talk on how he acquired this wonderful site. He bought the house for the house alone very cheaply and for the view down to the sea. Come the Spring he was attracted by patches of colour appearing in the wilderness down the valley and, upon investigation, quickly realised that his wilderness in the valley down to the sea had been in the dim and distant past a very complete, well-planted garden, with paths, ponds and rare and wonderful plants: mature and huge rhododendrons, azaleas, magnolias, all under-planted with primulas - a complete botanical paradise, but completely overgrown and obliterated by neglect and the passage of time. Some people have all the luck.

But it was an enormous challenge and undertaking to clear it all and restore it to its original glory. But this is what he did, involving an enormous amount of effort and hard work and no doubt expense, but eventually getting it back to a condition whereby he could open it up to the public, and so here we were, sharing his good fortune.

When he eventually reached the bottom of the valley, another surprise awaited him. On the beach was a large memorial stone, inscribed as follows:

To the Officers and Men of U.S. 29 Infantry Division

Who embarked from Trebah in June 1944

For the D-Day Assault on Omaha Beach, Normandy.

We Will Remember Them

It transpires that the US 29 Infantry Division trained on this remote beach with an overgrown garden and derelict house at the top of the valley, ideal for their purpose; but the story goes that one of the many wartime tragedies was enacted here as, during their training, 900 of them were killed by accident by their own forces. Sometime before our visit, the owner had a group of German visitors, so he addressed them in a similar manner to ourselves giving the history of the garden. When he had finished, one of the male members of the party spoke up, saying that he flew over this house and beach, no doubt while the US Infantry were on the beach and was going to bomb the house, but changed his mind because he thought it would be a nice house to acquire 'when they had won the war'. No doubt a good decision - if they had won the war.

However, if anyone is in this area in the future, this is a gem for all keen gardeners to seek out and spend an interesting and relaxing day. They have a restaurant where a good, full meal may be had or just light refreshments. There is also a good plant sale area where many unusual plants may be purchased. There is a large car park outside the entrance.

The coastline hereabouts has many similar inlets such as Trebah and similar gardens, but inland a great deal of interest may be found, such as derelict tin mines. These were very busy until the 1920s, but the tin ore is very deep, something like 4000 ft down. In the 1920-30s, tin was being found and surface-mined much more easily and more cheaply in Malaysia and elsewhere, which sounded the death knell for Cornish tin. A great pity as it is an old industry here - the Romans and Phoenicians came here for tin. Perhaps, with modern methods of mining it may return, as there are still considerable deposits of tin at 4000 ft, and beneath that there is copper and then more tin, but all very deep.

Fred Blount
December 14th 2000
Fred Blount Memoirs 13

More on Kettering Dust Destructor
by R.F. Blount

Since writing on this subject previously, I was a little concerned that perhaps I had not got all my facts and dates correct, so I visited the library and asked if they had any information or historical records on the subject, and was surprised and impressed by the immediate response that I was given.

Lots of dated facts and figures, detailed drawings dating from 1896, when Kettering Urban District Council applied to the Board of Trade for a provisional order, having considered this for some 10 years previously, owing to the town's expansion: shoe factories, houses and all the necessary shops and accompanying trades that went with the Shoe and Leather trades, including an explosion in population, estimated at this time to be approximately 30,000, along with an estimated 100 tons of rubbish per week, which at this time, was having to be transported to a suitable infill site over 2 miles out of town. So, the disposal of the town's rubbish along with the ever-increasing needs for power and light, the situation was becoming more and more desperate.

However, the provisional order was obtained in 1896, but several delays were experienced, so, Dr Kennedy was engaged in 1899, to prepare plans for a Dust Destructor and Electric Generator for a figure of £40,000 approximately, capable of handling and disposing of all the rubbish and generating power and lighting sufficient for the town's requirements. Several sites were considered, but eventually a site was purchased in 1903, by raising a loan for £43,000, for Dickmen's Orchard on the West side of Rockingham Road, with an entrance from Rockingham Road and a rear entrance from Field Street, and with an area of 7,377 square yards, considered large enough for the construction of the works envisioned at this time and according to Dr Kennedy's plans.

The work was put out to tender and nine tenders were received and eventually Messrs Meldrum Bros, were awarded the contract for a figure of £19,311-10s, for the provision of Lancashire steam boilers and refuse-burning equipment and all building associated with this equipment.

Later work was put in hand for other buildings and fencing, drainage, offices, etc. at a cost of £9,599-00s. Next, the chimney £1,597-00s and then Refuse Destructor Buildings £5,700-00s.

The chimney contained almost 1,000,000 bricks. Total cost of this building work was

£16,896-00s.

The above dates, facts and figures were taken from documents and papers in the Public Library and from a paper read at the District Meeting of the Incorporated Association of Municipal Engineers held at Kettering on September 2nd 1905. Title 'Electric Light and Power Station and Refuse Incinerator at Kettering' by Thos. Reader Smith.

The completed works became operational in May 1904. At this time, only half the available space was used, the rest was for future development as demand was required, both in the Boiler Room and Electrical Generator plant.

The boilers were fired with coal and refuse, burning 25 tons of refuse every 24 hours. Forced draught was supplied to ensure the complete destruction of all refuse by steam from the boilers being injected into the front of each boiler firebox.

This whole project was a massive undertaking at this time in Kettering's history, probably one of the momentous and forward-looking ventures in the town's history, which was borne out by visits by deputations from other towns and cities all over the country and Europe, with problems of rubbish disposal and electrical generation similar to ours.

From time to time, the plant was added to and capacity extended with demand. In 1923, extension of light and power to

Market Harborough, Desborough and Rothwell, Burton Latimer, Barton Seagrave and 19 other parishes were added to the load and so on, until about 1957-1960, when the grid system of electrical energy, power and light was introduced, and our wonderful plant was closed down.

No doubt, the power stations have given us a reliable network and system, but what has happened to our Dust Destructor and waste disposal system, the very serious item which our town planners for our future had introduced, looking to our future ongoing problems, like most of the rest of the country, dumping it into convenient landfill sites and covering it up, out of sight, out of mind. We cannot go on like this, the natural process is for nature to turn buried rubbish into noxious gases and for evermore rise to the surface, rendering it unsuitable as building land or any other useful purpose. You cannot bury rubbish.

And so, all that colossal expense at that time by our forebears, all their careful planning and forethought has gone and left us with the same problem that they started with and found the answer 100 years ago. One step forward and two steps backward. It is a world-wide problem with the same reasons and problems.

Last week, the Institute of Plumbers visited the Water Treatment Works at Crow Lane, Great Billing, Northampton, up to three years ago known as the Sewage Works for Northampton.

About three years ago, they extended this site and built a new Water Treatment Plant, installing the very latest equipment for handling sewage and turning it back into drinking water. Fortunately, the Water Board have done with our water supply what Kettering did with their rubbish problem in 1900, and in the last three years, have introduced the latest plant and methods of sewage handling and water purification, and increased and improved the capacity of the plant, largely by using the methane from the sewage to power the new plant and drive large pumps to increase the activation of the aerobic bacteria in the sewage, with the end result of good, clean water discharged back into the River Nene. Thank goodness, that the Water Board has dealt with this problem efficiently, because water is our life blood.

Unfortunately, the other part of our life blood is clean air, which so far has not been completely or satisfactorily addressed. In 1898, Kettering Urban District Council put a scheme in motion and at that time, addressed an urgent need for the disposal of our rubbish and at the same time, built an electricity generator, using coal and rubbish to fuel the boilers. This was a massive undertaking, involving raising a lot of money, but it was raised, some borrowed, some raised from shares in the project, but it was achieved and put into operation in 1904, as the result of a lot of confidence, careful planning, and courage, and all our rubbish was successfully disposed of in the best possible manner and continued to do so until about 1960. The only possible criticism that could be made with this system was the gases emitted from the chimney, which by this time would have been dealt with by the improvement in combustion, scrubbing the flue gases of carbon, sulphur, ammonia and others, until the escaping gases were mostly vapour. But sadly, we lost this wonderful plant when the electricity grid system arrived. Why it was dismantled, I do not know. By this time, it was serving a large area, apart from Kettering and must have been very remunerative. But the worst part was the fact that we now joined the rest of the country in burying our rubbish rendering large tracts of land unusable for building land or agriculture, as toxic gases are generated as soon as the rubbish is dumped, and will continue to do so for hundreds of years.

As I have mentioned earlier, a town in America about ten years ago, claimed they had found the perfect answer for disposal of rubbish and at the same time, generate electricity, and went on to describe the system that Kettering had recently dismantled. We urgently need to find an answer to this problem, otherwise we shall run out of ground and this small country will finish up as one huge rubbish dump.

The Kettering Dust Destructor was undoubtedly the most efficient system available. I suppose the initial cost would be high at today's rates, but Kettering faced up to this problem in 1898, and in my opinion, more and more of these schemes will eventually be the answer.

We are constantly being told of the existence of Radon gas in our houses and its dangers, but at the same time burying our rubbish and creating other gases that freely pollute the atmosphere. There is another problem that is being investigated at this moment in time, the incidence of cancer in communities and houses near power pylons. What would we do without electricity?

Perhaps, on the plus side of these problems is the fact that on some of the infill sites small businesses have developed, where plastics and glass are being separated, making useful products such as sheets of coloured plastic for various purposes and glass sheet and particles for garden use. This is good, to re-constitute rubbish into something useful, but it is a small percentage of our rubbish and it still leaves the rest that is buried.

Fred Blount
December 2000
Fred Blount Memoirs 14

The Accident
by R.F. Blount

In 1937, I bought my first car, a Morris 10/6 12 HP, 6-cylinder engine, from Harry Robinson, a well-known and respected motor engineer operating from a small garage in Weldon Street, Kettering. We tried it out, it smoked a bit and we decided it needed a re-bore and I agreed to purchase it, if he carried out a re-bore of the 6 cylinders and valves, for the asking price of £47-10s, and so I became the owner of my first car.

It was an interesting car, a luxury model, with all-leather upholstery, price new £225-00s, when you could buy a brand-new Ford 8 for £100 or a Morris 8 for £125-00s. But as we subsequently found out, the 6-cylinder engine was a failure, because the cylinders were too small and it lost speed and power on hills, a very smooth and comfortable ride, but it was not a success.

It was first registered in Middlesbrough VN 6302; the first owner was a man named Dixon, well-known as a speedway cyclist. I was the 4th owner in two years, which indicated that nobody was happy with it, but it served my purpose for 2 years, when my parents bought me a new Series E Morris 8, BBD 202, just before the war in 1939. This was the luxury model, 4-door, leather upholstery £145-00s, a nice car, my pride and joy for approximately 2 years.

We had been out for a Sunday afternoon run with my parents, returning home about 7.30 p.m., and in the middle of a heavy thunderstorm, to find my brother-in-law, Frank Billings and his wife Nellie and two-year-old son Stephen had visited us and were waiting for the rain to stop, so that they could return home and get Stephen to bed, so I took them home. This much I still remember, but the next thing I remember is waking up in the Kettering General Hospital on the following Wednesday. A policeman took a statement from me, goodness knows what I told him, but I think I learnt more from him than he did from me. First of all, I asked him where the accident had happened – the cross roads of St Mary's Road and Linden Avenue; there were three days of my life that I still have no recollection of. Apparently, I did not see the bus, and he hit me on the driving door, pushed me on the front of the bus until we hit the kerb, flattened me against the kerb, off the road and round a tree before coming to a stop.

Obviously, the bus's brakes were faulty, but when the people at the time found out that I had only third-party insurance, everyone lost interest. My first hard lesson on motor insurance; the best offer for the car remains was £15-00s, but a friend of the family gave me £17.10s as a favour, plus 8 months in hospital and a total of 53 weeks off work.

For 8 months, my wife came to visit me every evening, in all weathers. We had been married at that time for 6 months, when I had the accident.

A very poor start to our marriage. But I picked myself up and made a good recovery. Three years later, I started in business as a Plumber & Heating Engineer, with the help of my wife and parents.

About the end of 1945, things were beginning to progress and I needed transport. My friend Jack Payne suggested I put in a quote for an ex-P.O. van. So, acting on this, I visited the Kettering Post Office and a postman showed me the van for sale and he said, 'What do you think it is worth?' and carelessly I said, 'Oh, about £80.' It was sold for £85 to the postman!

So, the next van was at Wellingborough Post Office. The same drill as before, but when the postman asked me what it was worth, I replied 'I would not give more than £50 for it,' but put in a bid for £85 and so I obtained my first van: FGN 655, 117,000 miles on the clock and on its 4th engine, but it was built like a tank from 1/8 inch sheet aluminium body and thick rubber front mudguards, just the job for our purpose. I fitted a ladder rack to the roof and kept it for several years, with a final mileage of nearly 400,000 miles. Eventually, I had to get rid of it because I was the only one who would drive it, out of about 10 or 12 employees. The steering would rotate almost 360° before it engaged, also there was a leak on the radiator and I could not get a Morris Minor radiator. So, it was sold for £10-00s to Arthur Heath of Kettering Civic Society. I do not know what he did with it, but we certainly had our money's worth out of it. I shall have to ask him when I see him, what he did with it.

While I myself was still driving this van, the phone rang and the voice at the other end said, 'My wife has had an accident and run into the back of your van. Will you please inspect your van and let me know the cost of the damage?' At this time, I was living at 13 Roundhill Road, and the van was parked outside. It was daylight, but she was coming down London Road and turning into Roundhill Road; it is a bad corner, with the camber falling away a bit. She must have taken the corner too fast or something.

However, I inspected the van and I could see where she had hit the van; you could see the Post Office red paint showing through the grey where she had hit it, but otherwise nothing, so I returned to the phone and said, 'If you give me £2-10-00 we will call it quits.' Afterwards I felt guilty, because his wife's old Hillman Minx, as far as I could see, was a write-off. As I said earlier, it was built like a tank.

Another useful feature with the old Morris Minor was the thermometer on the filler cap, which was useful when the radiator developed a leak. As soon as the radiator overheated, the red hand in the thermometer would shoot up to the vertical boiling position. A bit old-fashioned, but I found it quite useful.

After this followed a succession of vans and cars, mostly new vehicles of various makes and sizes until eventually, we had a fleet of about 20 plus vans, plus cars. The last two new cars I bought were Citroen CX, no longer made, except to order as 'specials' at a price (?) but a beautiful car in every respect.

All vehicles after the accident were insured 'comprehensive'.

Fred Blount

January 2001

Fred Blount Memoirs 15

Holidays
by R.F. Blount

When I started my business as a Plumber & Heating Engineer, I made a strict rule which I kept up all my working life, to pay all my bills by the end of the month after receiving the statement. Also, the first 5 to 10 years, all profits were put into the business account.

By the mid-1950s, I made a further rule; I was working every minute, except Thursday evenings, when I went out with my friends and Saturday afternoons, when I always went out with my wife. This rule was to spend 2 weeks' holiday somewhere in the British Isles, and 2 weeks somewhere abroad. This way, we as a family had many interesting, happy, adventurous holidays every year.

The first trip abroad was about 1954, when we went to the South of France. We took the car, crossing by ferry from Dover to Calais, making our way South, passing the R101 Hotel on the site where the airship crashed, and stayed the first night in a small hotel in Montpellier, where we first experienced the use of duvet bed covers. Not being very familiar with this equipment, I was not very enthusiastic. The next day we headed South again, skirting Paris and calling in at Versailles Palace and on, heading towards the Jura mountains. We passed through a small town on a river where there was a may fly hatching; the flies lay about 6 inches deep on the road and on the windscreen, to an extent that I could not see to drive. The locals were out, filling linen bags, looking like pillow slips, with these flies; I never did find out what they did with them. Eventually, we ran out of this area affected by the flies.

The roads in this northern part of France were lined with trees, looking like some form of poplar, but they were all loaded with mistletoe. All these roads at this time, impressed me, having no kerbs and also a hard shoulder on both sides of the road about

6 feet wide, so that anyone in any sort of trouble or difficulty, could run off the road safely at all times.

The roads were also fairly straight. I remember on one occasion, travelling for about 20 miles along a straight road which eventually, appeared to be going up into the sky. But as we progressed, I could see it was a church steeple which had obviously been used as a marker for the road and having passed through the town, the road continued again straight for some distance.

Eventually, we reached the Jura's and on passing through the area renowned for making scent from flowers and somewhere here we saw a large rock, covered with cyclists' names where the Tour de France had apparently had a resting place. Shortly after this, we hit the coast near Nice and passed through Cannes to our destination, Agay. The only problem was that when we presented ourselves at our hotel, they had misunderstood our letter and had bookings for us two weeks later, or that was their story anyhow. I never did quite understand their reasoning or story. So, remembering passing a large hotel, we returned to this hotel and were received by an old lady dressed in black, reminding me of my grandmother in the early 1920s. We explained our difficulties, but she said they were full up. We had David and Margaret with us aged about 9 and 7, and she was looking at them and finally said wait here and she would try to help. Off she went and eventually returned, saying that there was an attic room with one double bed, and she could make up a bed on the floor for the children, which we gratefully accepted. We had our meals with the other guests and fared very well, but I myself did not care much for the French Riviera. We had three days of the Mistral, sand and wind; sand got everywhere, in the eyes, in your food, everywhere. A section of the beach belonged to the hotel, and any other beach had to be paid for. Forest fires raged the whole time a few miles inland, with a constant smell of smoke in the air. We had a look round at the adjoining coastal towns, Cannes, Saint-Tropez, Nice, but, as I have said, I was not particularly attracted to the area. The farming in this southern part of France was still rather primitive, ploughing and carts being pulled by oxen. Nora would have gone again, but we finally went to Spain the next year, motoring through France by a different route.

Before we left for Spain, I wrote to the AA for a route taking us through the Pyrenees via Andorra; they wrote back with the route, but warning us not to go through the Pyrenees as the roads were still blocked with snow at the end of May. I was disappointed and followed the route as far as the foothills of the Pyrenees. We stopped at a hotel, which was also a spa for rheumatic diseases, and when we were having dinner, a Frenchman on the next table came across saying did we mind if he sat at our table, because he was in the 8th Army during the war and learnt some English and wished to exercise his English. He joined us and went on to explain that he was there for treatment and lived about 40 miles away. I told him of the AA warning regarding blocked roads, to which he immediately replied that the roads had been cleared three days previously.

So, we carried on. The roads had been cleared, but there was a wall of snow on one side and torrents of water were coming across the road from melting snow; eventually, we came to a section of the road that was partly washed away, leaving a car's width. We stopped and I looked at it carefully; it was almost impossible to turn round anyway and eventually, I tackled it and succeeded. Eventually, we reached the frontier post which was also the highest point of the road, and at this time, was still a dirt road 2000 metres or about 6500 feet above sea level and from this point it was all downhill into Andorra. Breathtakingly beautiful, hairpin bends and although dirt roads, expertly banked and at the same time losing as much incline as possible, had to take them very slowly and carefully; it was like falling into a hole with the car almost standing on end. When we left the last town on the French side, the roses in the flower beds were all in full bloom, but as we got higher in the Pyrenees and down to Andorra, the flowers went back to early Spring, miles and miles of narcissi, and when we stopped for lunch, we put our bottles of lemonade in the snow to cool it. I wandered off down the hillside with my camera, taking pictures (colour slides): primulas, polyanthus, gentians and lots of other flowers; azalea bushes were in bud and so on.

We eventually tore ourselves away from this natural beauty and went on our way. We saw a man walking down the middle of the road with what looked like a carpenter's rush tool bag over his shoulder. He bent down, depositing the contents of the bag into a hole in the road: stones, which he levelled with his foot, went to the roadside and filled the bag with more stones and moved on to the next hole in the road; he was the road-mender. Shortly after this, we overtook a donkey and cart. We stopped to take pictures. The driver jumped down off the cart and posed for us, saying 'Typical'. The donkey had a straw hat on its head with the ears sticking up through the hat. About here there were golden eagles circling high above.

Eventually, we arrived at and passed through Andorra and down into Spain and eventually arriving at a ski resort, Puigcerda, where we ran into one of their wonderful festivals. First of all, a policeman in white uniform and pith helmet, directing traffic at a cross-roads entering the town; he held up the traffic and waved us on. I said to Nora, 'Look they are expecting us.' It was an agricultural area and tractors were parked on the outskirts of the town, towing floats of flowers: gladioli, carnations, asters, all colours. One that clearly remains in my memory was a huge swan about 30 ft high. All the streets were festooned with paper decorations. We found a hotel and had a meal, and then went out to join in the festivities.

We eventually found that it was all about a festival of 'Julie the Witch' and in the evening a carriage and horses, with an effigy of Julie in the open carriage, with some local beauties as her attendants, finally arriving at a park with a lake and island, where Julie was burnt with a magnificent firework display. A wonderful experience, and completely unexpected. The shops were open until about midnight, and I bought a straw sun hat at about 10.30 p.m., which still hangs in the garage, dirty and battered, but it brings back happy memories.

The next day, we were on our way again, going down into Spain via Gerona, passing through an area where roofing tiles and bricks were made, lots of chimneys all bent away from the sun, the constant heat from the sun on the south side giving them all a lean northward. Also in this area were a lot of potteries, where we bought and still have some interesting, coloured plates, some decorated with fish or flowers, etc. When we later re-visited Gerona, a large town, we bought a small chair with sea-grass seat for about 50 pts. This we still have in the kitchen. They work in the mornings, siesta till about 5 p.m., and then work in the evenings. We were walking along a back street with some windows at floor level and looking through an open window, they were having an evening lunch break and a young chap caught my eye and held up his leather wine bottle to me; I smiled and nodded and then walked on. I had not moved many yards when I heard a shout and turning round, there he was with his leather bottle of wine. So, I went back and successfully had a refreshing drink of his wine. You do not put the metal top in your mouth, but hold it, you squeeze the bottle and catch the jet of wine in your mouth. I had had a little practice at this and he applauded my success; I suppose he was expecting me to make a mess of it. But they were all nice, sociable people.

Eventually, we reached our destination, Calella, on the Mediterranean coast. These drives through the Pyrenees were very pleasant and memorable.

We were on the beach one day and a storm came on, heavy rain. There were arches under the road, most of them housing boats, but one arch was open like a bridge, so we dived for this. After a few minutes, we heard a shout and, looking out, a few arches along the beach a man was working on his boat and he was beckoning us urgently to join him; after about ten minutes, he drew our attention to the arch where we had been sheltering. There was a roaring torrent coming through it and across the beach into the sea.

We visited Palafrugell about two miles inland on market day, where they blocked the main street with a cart at each end and spread their wares, vegetables, fruit, etc. on the road in heaps. Huge green watermelons like footballs, 4 pts each. These we tried; they were lovely: rich orange flesh, juicy and sweet. The shops, general stores and wine shops, were interesting. The wine shops, huge wine casks; the drill is to taste them all and then have a leathern bottle of the one you like, very cheap. Plums or prunes, pressed into a huge block on the counter, all sold by the kilo in a similar manner that they used to sell dates here in the 1920s and 1930s. We also tried this, and it was similar to very thick plum jam: very nice.

We attended an interesting evening's entertainment, actually one of the best examples of dancing I have ever seen in my life, a complete surprise. We booked and occupied a table on which were glasses and a bottle of champagne, not very good, reminding me of paraffin, but this was made up for by the entertainment which followed. There was a gipsy caravan parked by the side of the hotel and eventually, a whole family of real Spanish gipsies emerged and commenced the entertainment of <u>real</u> Spanish country dancing; they were all good but the man, who I took to be the father was far better than good: he was magnificent. The family dancers were a mixture of country dancing with good footwork and castanets all brightly dressed, typically Spanish colourful dress, the man was tall and very lean and his footwork was the essence of the show. The family provided the music with string instruments and he started off with loud tap-dancing, and then gradually the music went quieter and quieter, until you could only hear the tapping from his feet, also becoming quieter with the music and the number of taps to the second was unbelievable, and then becoming louder and louder again. It was a wonderful evening and wonderful entertainment. The following year we visited the same hotel and event again, hoping to see the gipsies again, but we were very disappointed. The dancers were a group of professionals from Barcelona; they just were not in the same category as the gipsies. If we had not seen the real thing the previous year, no doubt we would have enjoyed it.

One day we went to Barcelona to the Bull Fight. We finally found ourselves suitable seats in the magnificent and impressive arena. This first year, this all happened in the afternoon, the early part of June, before it was too hot and we had an interesting day watching the various events. Towards the end, about 6 pm, it became obvious that a thunderstorm was brewing. We made our way back to the car and just made it before the storm broke.

Off we went, it was about 100 miles to Calella and we were running short of petrol. All this part of Northern Spain was supplied with electricity from hydro-electric plants in the Pyrenees and when a storm broke, these plants often broke down and, on this occasion, the supply had failed; all the towns we passed through were in darkness and so were the petrol pumps. We were getting desperate for petrol but eventually, came to a small town, lit obviously with their own generator and we obtained petrol and eventually, arrived at Calella. The only other event was that there were a lot of pigeons flying around in the Bull Ring and one bombed me a direct hit, ran all down my face: they have large pigeons in Barcelona.

When we went home, we obtained some food to eat on the journey, accompanied with a good bottle of champagne. We stopped and enjoyed some of this refreshment at lunch time; Nora and I had a drop of champagne, the children had some orange drink. We corked the champagne and off we went. We had not gone far when 'pop' the cork came out of the bottle. Well, it was too good to waste, so I drank the remains of 1 litre of champagne. Off we went again, like a dose of salts, through the Pyrenees. We went back by a different route, via a different frontier post, where the authorities had a large American Packard car, which they had obviously recognised or else the driver had been rude and upset them. They had all the removable upholstery out all over the road, the wheel hub caps off, the bonnet up, spare wheel out; they were having the time of their lives, giving it a real going-over and as we left, it looked as if they left it to the owner to put his car together again. It is good practice to exercise one's best behaviour at these frontier posts.

On the way back through France, we passed through a town in the wine area with a refreshment bar in the shape of a large barrel. We took refreshment here and while we were thus engaged, we were entertained by an Auto Circus. The centre of the town was roped off and apparently the Circus were having a practice run for the performance in the evening. They had some battered saloon cars, which they drove at speed up ramps to turn them over, and roll them over and over down the centre of the road. The other trick they were doing was to drive on to a ramp and on to two wheels, and driving between an avenue of trees on two wheels for about 200 yards.

Having watched this, we were late getting back on our journey, with about 350 miles to do and about 3½ to 4 hours to catch our ferry. So, we made a mad dash back via Lyon and a tunnel under the city. Thank goodness, for the long straight stretches of road in France. We just made it, to complete another interesting and eventful holiday.

We returned to Calella for two or three years, to the same guest house, run by a Seňor Sapera and his wife, elderly people, and I was impressed by his command of the English language, and one day, I asked him about this and he explained that in his younger days, he used to visit London quite frequently in his capacity as a grain merchant, but after General Franco had taken over, his life style, by necessity, had changed. For instance, he had lived in Barcelona and this large property in Calella had been his country residence, but under the new regime, he had to open it up as a guest house. He and his wife were very nice people, and we had some pleasant holidays with them.

But having said all this, the popular and general opinion of the Spanish people was that General Franco had done a good job for Spain and the Spanish people and looking back, I think he was probably, the best of all the dictators at this time, taking the crown prince and educating him to take over the running of the country.

I have vivid memories of an old woman on the beach, with her Spanish guitar, playing 'Valencia' not very well and her voice was not any better, and always the same tune.

Fred Blount

January 2001

Fred Blount Memoirs 16

Our Life Blood – Drinking Water
by R.F. Blount

In my early working days, I became keenly interested in drinking water and its quality, from 1929 onwards, when I found out that at that time, 4 parts per million of chlorine approximately, was added to our mains water to make it safe and allowing for some degree of impurities.

My first sharp and memorable experience was at 80 Princes Street, Kettering, where I lived with my parents. I was 14 years old in 1929, having just started work as a plumber's mate: no fancy frills like apprenticeships then, I came home for my midday meal 12.30 to 1.30, and went out with a glass jug to the pump in the yard, which served us as drinking water, shared between three houses, normally beautiful water, ice-cold in the summer, from a fairly deep well, fed by a natural spring, in the centre of our garden covered with a York stone slab about 1 ft 6 in, deep under the garden soil.

But this particular day, the water was not its usual crystal-clear colour, but cloudy and milky-coloured. Fortunately, as I have said, it was a glass jug and having already learnt a little about blocked drains, etc. I became suspicious and smelt the jug's contents and received an instant sewage smell. I took the water in to my parents, who confirmed my suspicions. Between us we lifted the York stone slab over the interceptor trap, where the main drain left the property to join the main sewer and it was full to the top with sewage, and had made its way into our drinking water.

My parents immediately reported the situation to the town's Sanitary Inspector, Mr Duce, who promptly came and confirmed our complaint and duly condemned our drinking water supply, and at the same time, made arrangements for a main water supply and flushing cisterns and modern WCs, which was much appreciated after the old long drop and filthy bucket system, which was operated when water from the kitchen sink passed under the w.c., turning over a hinged bucket: not very hygienic, but one step in the right direction. Shortly after, the builder arrived, George Knight of Commercial Road, Kettering, whom I eventually did a lot of work with, when I started my own business: Alf Knight, Bob Knight and a builder's labourer, Harry Matcham.

When they had finished, we had a safe water supply and the luxury of a modern, flush toilet.

Some years after this, Knights were carrying out some alterations to the vaults of the Westminster Bank and somehow Harry Matcham was locked in the vault, by mistake, and had to remain so, as two keyholders were required to release him and one had gone home. But eventually, he was released, none the worse for his experience.

Again, about this time, I was sent to repair a ball valve in the tank in the roof of a house in Weekley occupied by Mr & Mrs Walker, about 1935 or 1936, when Mr Walker was Manager or Chief Engineer of the Kettering Electricity Works. Nice people, we always had a cup of tea and home-made cakes when working there.

When I repaired the ball valve in the tank, I was surprised to see several dead birds floating on top of the tank in various states of decay, and lots of bones on the bottom of the tank. I advised them to get the tank boxed in with a lid on the top, but it has always remained in my memory, and I have always been very careful not to use the hot tap for drinking purposes.

Many years later, about 1960, after I had started in business myself and doing a great deal of work around Northamptonshire County Council properties including schools, I was called to unblock a tap in Henry Gotch Senior School kitchen. A cold-water tap was blocked and on removing the top of the tap, I found it to be blocked with feathers. These I removed and remembering past experiences, I immediately climbed the vertical steel ladder to the tank inside the top of the water tower. It was a large tank with a 3-inch ball valve and 4-inch overflow pipe, passing straight out through the outer wall. I was amazed at what I had found: pigeons, jackdaws and a selection of smaller birds all floating on the surface and the bottom of the tank was two or three inches deep with feathers and bones.

When I returned to the kitchen, I was considering what I should do about this, as this was one of hundreds of similar schools we maintained in the County, and realised that I could be starting a large problem if it was reported. However, the situation was settled by a curious coincidence. I was inspecting the rest of the taps for blockage or leaking washers and while I was doing this, the N.C.C. Schools' Canteen Inspector turned up to do her routine inspection. Eventually, she came over and asked me what the third tap was for, over the wash basin at the end of the preparation tables; this basin is used to wash the hands between different vegetables, etc. This was the opportunity I had been looking for, so I told her this was a drinking water tap. She looked surprised and turned round and said, so what are these other taps, where the staff were in the habit of filling the orange juice drinks from. She began to look interested so I kept going, telling of the tap blocked with feathers and my subsequent inspection of the tank and its contents, and from then on painted as lurid a description as I could. In for a penny, in for a pound. What would the N.C.C. say? I thought it was time it was all brought to light.

When I had finished, she nearly hit the roof. I then went on to explain that the drinking water tap in question was the only drinking water tap in the building, plus two drinking fountains, one on the ground floor and one on the first floor. The kitchen, Domestic Science Rooms, Cooking Rooms, Staff Rooms, etc. were all tank-fed.

She went to find the Head and told him what I had told her, and soon the whole school was in uproar. Shortly after this, all the tanks had lids fitted to them all round the County, but this was not much good because the birds were getting into the tanks through the overflow pipes, still under the lids.

However, since this time, building regulations have changed, also water supply regulations have changed to take these problems into consideration. It seems quite obvious that all cold-water taps will be supplied direct from the main water supply.

But talking about water and the many complications we manufacture as we blindly stagger forward in our ignorance, through what we call progress (?), I have just returned from a most interesting and educational visit to China, concentrated on the world's most powerful river, the Yangtze. Only the third longest river, but unquestionably, the most powerful and up till now claiming thousands of lives most years in its flood waters, but more of that later.

About the same time as the Henry Gotch School episode, 1960 or thereabouts, we were getting reports about a comparatively new killer disease, Legionnaires' Disease, which again was traced back to the storage tanks in large hotels and other large buildings. Was there a connection here with birds or small vermin getting into the tanks? The circumstances were very similar. Legionnaires' Disease, which I know nothing about and therefore, have to leave it to specialists in Health Departments to deal with, but after what I myself saw and brought to light at the Henry Gotch School, one school in Kettering, where there were and still are many other schools and similar tanks and water supply systems, it does require a great deal of careful thought and action to correct these mistakes and oversights, flaws in our ways of thinking and way forward.

Since 1960, in my travels round the world and this country, my eyes automatically pick out buildings with a tank room at the highest part of the building or on the roof, and find myself thinking how many dead birds are there polluting the water systems or how long before we put all these mistakes right.

But through all this, there is a reassurance that our own water supply from the mains, with the elementary 4 parts chlorine to 1 million parts of water, plus rest of the water treatment these days, was obviously sufficient to keep the water safe, even with all the decomposed birds and feathers and sundry impurities in our water, at that time. But it does not do to become complacent, or take for granted our water supplies and sewage disposal; the two go and work hand in hand, and it is our duty to observe and report, especially the plumber, to report any abnormality he observes.

Even with the added chlorine at that time, that building and thousands of similar buildings must have been close to epidemic outbreaks. So again, was there a connection with Legionnaires' Disease? Were there any dead birds or foreign bodies?

These tanks at this time, around 1960, were always out of sight and out of mind, a very serious situation, only seen on rare occasions by the plumber, who was attracted to their isolated position by some rare fault in the water supply system and as I see it, was responsible to report any abnormality he saw on these occasions. Plumbing, I have found to be a very interesting, important and responsible job, important regarding the health of the community in general terms.

So, time goes on, we learn by our mistakes and make the occasional correction, but one mistake we have not addressed in my opinion yet, and that is pollution in its many forms, mainly still burying our rubbish, so very wrong. With all our education and degrees in every subject, we have not yet found a satisfactory answer to this all-important problem, other than burying it out of sight, out of mind, leaving it to nature to convert it back into gases and released back into the atmosphere, slowly but surely, converting this small island into one massive rubbish dump, the very land being rendered useless for growing our crops or for building.

I have just returned from a holiday in China, a country which up to the early part of the 20th century, resisted all efforts by the western world to bring in the modern improvements, such as railways and other modern transport, telephone, electricity and also, they resisted the entrance of explorers and plant collectors, such as Chinese Wilson, Kingdom Ward, Robert Fortune, their entrances and work carried out mostly in the Himalayan areas under great risk and difficulty, and when these areas were still frequented by and travellers met with , Chinese bandits. But at this time and also up to now, for thousands of years and their civilisation, going back to about 6000 BC, the Chinese who have lived on or near the banks of the Yangtze have dumped all their rubbish in the river, successfully, with no ill effects because of the vast volume of water that comes down from the glaciers and peaks of the Himalayas, and carried out to the delta of that immense waterway. What the rest of China does with its rubbish I do not know, but certainly along the banks of the Yangtze so far, they had a simple answer to one of our most difficult problems, but after the new dam and hydro-electric scheme is complete, this old habit will be removed or prohibited.

Fred Blount
17th June 2001
Fred Blount Memoirs 17

Sunday January 27th 2001
by R.F. Blount

When I was 8 years old, I joined the St Mary's Church Choir. Father Glaister was the Vicar at this time, Sid Loasby was the Organist and Choirmaster and also there was a pillar of the church, a Mr George Hanger, who was employed by one of the Kettering shoe factories during the week, but on Sundays was the equivalent of a curate or assistant priest, read the gospels and lessons and also chanted the 'Graduals' each week.

Since the introduction of the new prayer book and form of service, I have complained to friends regarding the alteration in the service as I could no longer recognise it, or if you like, recite it from memory, as I had done all my life without referring to the weekly leaflet, giving the readings and also the 'Gradual'. Quite suddenly, during this morning's service, my eyes picked up the word 'Gradual' Psalm 48, and my memory flashed back to the early days of my church life at St Mary's Church and George Hanger chanting the 'Gradual'. I had not recognised it because the music was different, at that time we were using the English Hymnal, the same as we use now, but the hymns numbered from 1 to 500 and something, and then continuing to 600 and something for the 'Graduals'. All of them numbered after the hymns, within the English Hymnal. So, our present service has reverted to the form of service used in the 1920s and Father Hanger's chanting, and lots of other happy memories of my early days, and my wife's at St Mary's Church. Happy days!

Fred Blount
January 2001
Fred Blount Memoirs 18

China and the Yangtze
by
Fred Blount

<u>Day 1. The Journey Out and Flight Details, Route, etc.</u>

We departed from Heathrow on June 15th 2001 at 12.30 p.m., by Virgin Atlantic. Meals were served, including a small bottle of red wine, very good.

On the back of the seat in front of you was a small television screen and a headset control on the arm of each seat. I tried the various channels, but like all television, some interesting, some boring, depending upon your taste or interest, but there was one programme which caught my interest and which I periodically switched over to, and that was a map of our journey, with a small plane marking our progress and flight details. I found a piece of paper and jotted down on it various details as we progressed. I was curious as to what route we would be taking. The following are my notes:

>We headed off over the North Sea
>Copenhagen, 600 mph ground speed
>St Petersburg, Yetersburg
>Valdayskaya Alps, Outside air temperature -70°, Altitude 37,000 ft
>Ural Mountains
>Western Siberia Lowlands
>Novosibirsk, Irkutsk
>Sayan Mountains
>Tibet/Mongolia
>Ulan Bator
>Beijing
>Shanghai, 4800 miles, flying time 11 hours
>Chongqing

We arrived at Pu-Dong Airport, Shanghai and boarded a bus which took us to the Equatorial Hotel next door to the Hilton Hotel, where Peace Talks were in progress while we were there – both top-class hotels.

The new Shanghai Airport was of fantastic design, being recently opened and they say, in an effort to influence China's effort to secure the venue for the World Olympics 2008. The very latest in every way, very impressive, from a distance taking on the appearance of a huge seagull. This part is at the moment only ¼ complete. Other associated building is to follow.

<u>Day 2</u>. The stay at the hotel was only for one night. The next day, we were taken by coach to the old Shanghai Airport, where we boarded another plane to take us to Chongqing and again, we stayed one night in the Harbour Plaza Hotel. In the afternoon, we were given a sightseeing tour of the town and a visit to a silk factory, mulberry bushes, silk worms, cocoons, and machinery and looms weaving the silk into thread and silk material and products. Also, a visit to a Chinese garden, 'The Humble Administrator's Garden', with lotus ponds on four sides of a central pavilion.

The next day, we embarked on the Victoria cruise ship, which in effect was a floating hotel, and our hotel for the next five days, cruising 1500 miles down the Yangtze River. It is the third largest river in the world, rising high up in the Himalayan Mountains, rushing and tearing its way down to Shanghai and the sea and over thousands of years, forming deep and spectacular gorges on the way, heavily loaded with sand and mud, constantly resembling a milk chocolate river.

China is the third largest country in the world with a surface area of 3,705,000 square miles and a population estimated at 1,114,000,000. Before we left Shanghai, we were given a coach trip to the Humble Administrator's Garden, already described, after which we boarded a river boat which took us down a canal off the Yangtze, The Suzhou Creek, which meanders through part of old Shanghai's suburbs, with spectacular arched bridges crossing the canal at intervals, in some places houses built right down to the canal banks and in other parts beautiful gardens down to the banks. Suzhou is very beautiful with the gardens full of exotic trees and shrubs lining the canal banks and popularly known as 'The Venice of the East'.

The Humble Administrator's Garden and its fabled Western Lake with its lotus blossoms, bridges, pagodas and temples is also within the Shanghai suburbs.

The Chinese make good use of the beauty of flowers in their language: Shanghai means 'Above the Sea' and 'Flower' is a euphemism for a prostitute and 'Sing-Song' houses, a well- and long-established trade in China, with names such as 'The House of Sure Satisfaction' or 'The Hall of Beauties'. All are associated with good eating and opium smoking which also at this time is on the decline. I suppose with our present-day attitudes to drugs and their evils and the like.

Day 3 of our holiday was taken up mostly by the flight up to Chongqing but in the late afternoon and evening, we enjoyed a coach tour of the city and one of the many markets and then back to the boat and evening meal. I was a little concerned before the holiday regarding the food as I am a diabetic, but I found no problems – plenty of good appetising food and the main menu was perfectly satisfactory for diabetics. I think we eat far too much sweet food in our Western diets.

Day 4. We commenced our 1500-mile trip down the Yangtze, including a Captain's Welcome Cocktail Party and finally mooring at Fengdu and Pingdusan Mountain, said to be the abode of devils with hundreds of temples dedicated to gods of the underworld.

Right from our arrival in China, I was impressed by the Chinese – their good manners and attention, especially if, like myself, walking with the aid of a stick they were all attention and giving all the attention they could; early on I tried to give a taxi man a tip, but he looked horrified and shook his head vigorously from which I concluded that tipping was not allowed.

Today, a trip up to a mountain village was arranged, but to take part it involved crossing a floating pontoon bridge, a series of wooden planks on boats across the Yangtze about ¼ mile, after which was a flight of 100+ steps up to the road where the coach was parked. I was a bit doubtful about all those steps, but our tour operative had sorted this out and produced a sedan chair and four Chinese porters. I sat in the chair and was carried across the pontoon and up a zig-zag path up the opposite bank to the coach. We finally reached our village after a pleasant ride only to be faced with another flight of steps – 40 they said, but when we came back, we counted 76. However, two of our fellow holiday companions grabbed one each of my arms and assisted me up and down. The village was interesting. We had our midday meal and had a look around the shops and mini-market, and then back to our floating hotel and evening meal.

Day 5 The Three Small Gorges. The Qutang and Wu gorges; the first Qutang is the shortest, but the more spectacular, the Wu gorge passes beneath 12 mountain peaks.

The gorges, they say, were formed about 70 million years ago, when an earth movement caused the drainage of a vast inland sea. But whatever it was, it has formed an awe-inspiring spectacle, but a bit disappointing from the photographer's point of view, inasmuch as from the gorge you just cannot get it all in a photograph. We had to transfer to smaller boats to negotiate these gorges. Again, we stopped and had to climb a series of steps for our midday meal.

Day 6 The Three Gorges and Dam. The San Dou Ping Dam will, when completed, be the world's largest dam creating a reservoir 390 miles long and up to 575 feet deep. We passed by this partially-completed in the third Xiling Gorge which is about

45 miles long. When completed, it will be equipped with a single lift lock for smaller ships and a stair of 5 locks for larger vessels and the water will eventually rise an amazing 361 feet above its present normal level, submerging farms, villages, steel works, and coal mines along its banks.

Farms and smallholdings are being re-housed on higher ground. Some of those properties we passed through on some of our excursions were in a very poor condition and therefore, any form of move along with water supply and sanitation has got to be an improvement. It is a 17-year project estimated at a cost of 13.5 billion dollars and a displacement of 1.2 million people. But all the world's largest civil engineers are anxious to get a piece of the action and all the leading countries to invest money into it – the largest dam and reservoir and the largest hydro-electric scheme in the world, and when completed probably, the largest profit producer to its investors.

<u>Day 7</u>. After leaving the dam, we cruised along a more tranquil length of the Yangtze, towards Wuhan, one of China's largest cities and capital of Hubei province, largely involved in steel production. We docked and were taken on a city sightseeing tour of Wuhan and then back for dinner on the ship.

The popular reason or excuse for the massive undertaking of the dam is the regular flooding of the Yangtze and each time it happens, the colossal loss of life and also the massive generating of power, and water supply, and irrigation to adjoining food-production farming.

<u>Day 8</u>. We left Wuhan and proceeded on our journey towards Juijiang, where we again were taken by coach to the top of Mount Lushan, a breathtaking trip with beautiful views of the forest below. We stopped and saw tea plants growing and then continued to the top, where there was a palace which Mao Zedong (Mao Tse-tung) used for important political meetings of the Central Committee of the Communist Party 1959-1970.

Day 9. We sailed downstream overnight to the port of Wuhu. These trips downstream were uneventful and a little disappointing inasmuch as although, there was a great deal of traffic on the river, it was largely uninteresting: steel, modern vessels with a diesel engine at the back end and very little by way of light showing. Sometimes, we were awakened by a powerful blast of the ship's siren in the middle of the night, indicating that some vessel or the other was in the way. I was disappointed that we did not see a single Chinese junk sailing boat.

We arrived at the port of Wuhu, went ashore to board a coach which took us to Mount Heargshan, which means 'Yellow Mountains', the name of a vast 72 peak range of mountains, part of Anhui province. The highest peak is 5904 feet high. Most of these peaks are accessible by means of stone steps. Unfortunately, I was unable to make this trip, as the altitude would have given me trouble with my pacemaker. Some of our party did it and travelled by coach to a cable car, which takes you to the summit in 15 minutes and, at the top, the summit is a further 10 minutes climb, for which you can buy a bamboo walking stick for about ten shillings (or 50p). I would have liked to have gone on this trip, but not a good place to be taken ill with altitude sickness.

Day 10. Nanjing is one of China's most beautiful natural areas, among lakes and rivers and wooded areas. It is also famous for its double-deck bridge carrying the Beijing to Shanghai railway, and also a main road. This bridge was initially to be built by Russian contractors, who agreed to design and supply the engineering skill and the steel, but after 3 years of talks and doubts regarding whether it would withstand the enormous floods of the river, eventually, China decided to take the work from the Russians and to do it all themselves. In 1960, they commenced work on the bridge and completed it in eight years. It is 1 mile long, top level is the road and the lower level for rail. We passed under this bridge on our last day down the river to Shanghai.

Day 11. Back in Shanghai, where some of our party flew back home, but we had an extended stay in Shanghai for another 5 days.

During Days 1 and 2 when we first arrived in Shanghai, we were taken on a coach tour along the main highway – a new road similar and equal to our M1, with three lanes separated by a middle reservation, planted with shrubs. On either side of the motorway, as far as the eye could see, was intense cultivation with an approximately 24-inch water main with periodical branch take-offs and valves to irrigate this huge horticultural enterprise, producing vast quantities of vegetables and food, also fish farms, all very highly organised and on a very large scale, very impressive. In this area, close to the Yangtze, water is one commodity that they are never short of, and they obviously are making maximum use of it. The coach trip along this road was about 1½ hours each way. Just outside Shanghai, we passed through a complicated road junction, recently completed, equal to our Spaghetti Junction and if anything, larger and more complex. Very impressive as all the new developments in China appear to be.

There is one thing that they have not yet tackled and that is air pollution in the cities. The air in Shanghai is so heavily polluted that you can taste it; everything you touch has a coating of carbon, filthy, but with all the new buildings it looks clean. However, if air pollution is not tackled quickly and effectively, it will soon take on a dingy appearance.

On the day that our holiday commenced, a book was dropped through the letter box. I picked it up and upon a quick inspection, I could see no obvious evidence as to who had sent it, so I dropped it in my suitcase and fetched it out on our arrival in Shanghai. On the second page, a blank page, was a written message revealing that my new next-door neighbour had sent this book, all about the Yangtze River and 'The River at the Centre of the World', by Simon Winchester, a very interesting book dealing with the history of the country, its people and the river and its long history and civilisation, going back to about 6000 BC: 8000 years with its many troubles and trials.

The invasion in the 1930-40s by Japan, who at that time considered themselves the master race and occupied part of China, Manchuria, using whole towns and areas and their occupants for research on all the known diseases and poisons and their reactions to them – far worse than the Western world ever used animals in this way. This all came to an end when they were eventually defeated at the end of the Second World War. Ever since then, they have been very carefully watched and controlled and thankfully, their activities restricted. But what happened to the results of all this?

Fred Blount

October 2001

Fred Blount Memoirs 19

Singapore, Pacific Islands, Bali, Komodo, Australia, Bangkok

by R.F. Blount

<u>1st Day</u>.   Depart Heathrow January 4th 1995 – 16:05

Arrive at Singapore January 5th – 12:55

Air conditioning in the aircraft and the walkway from the aircraft to reception and the passport area. All very cool and comfortable. All flat surface areas covered with a magnificent show of Orchids: Dendrobiums, Vandas and others. Our passports were duly examined, and we passed from the airport building into the street and it was so hot, it left me gasping for breath. But we only had to cross the road to our bus, waiting to transport us to our hotel and to my relief, we were back in a refrigerated cool atmosphere and we subsequently found out that this was the situation wherever you went in Singapore. You only had to step into the nearest building or form of transport and you were in an air-conditioned environment.

Leaving the airport, we passed down an avenue of Robinia Fan Palms, Vadola Double Coconut (Ladies Bottom Palms), their trunks having this shape and appearance.

We eventually reached our hotel, Shangri-La. Very good and very comfortable, but I could not sleep as it was too cool and I had to find an overlay to get warm. In the morning, I altered the room thermostat to up the temperature a bit.

<u>2nd Day</u>. January 6th. We went round the gardens in the morning, rated as second only to the Botanic Gardens in Singapore and met Roy Lancaster half way round, enjoying this wonderful garden. Later, we had a conducted tour of Singapore Botanic Gardens, our bus being escorted by police motorcycles to the gardens, where we were met by the Curator who gave us a conducted tour of the gardens, telling us the history of the gardens and the research carried out there and the details of the

trees and plants that we saw. This special treatment was no doubt due to the presence of Roy Lancaster, the organiser of this trip.

The conducted tour continued through the many sections and we finally reached the Orchid section, which held a special interest for me, but all varieties growing happily outdoors, where we struggle to get ours to grow indoors with special equipment, humidifiers and mist sprayers, to achieve the near perfect conditions. After having a good look at all the Vandas, Phalaenopsis, Dendrobiums, Cattleyas and many others, growing quite happily in the steamy hot atmosphere of Singapore, we were taken to a pavilion at this end of the garden for refreshments and photographs, after which we went back to the entrance where we were taken into a group of buildings where plant research laboratories were grouped, the workings of which were briefly explained to us.

After this, we were taken back to our hotel for our evening meal, but the next day we returned to the Botanic Gardens to have a more leisurely look around. Later this same day, we had a tour of the city, shops and markets and also visiting Raffles Hotel, where as all visitors do, we had a Gin Sling. It is a wonderful building, everything is in white marble: staircases, walls, floor, gardens, everything - all very cool. Close by, near the water front, is a large white marble statue of Raffles.

<u>3rd, 4th and 5th Days</u>. January 7th, 8th and 9th. We embarked on the Marco Polo, our cruise liner and commenced our cruise through the group of islands, the Indonesian group of islands, on our way to the next port of call, Bali. There are something in the order of 8500 islands in this group. We were most of this time in sight of some land or other, all looking very much like extinct volcanoes. We landed at Bali, and were taken to a village and were entertained by the islanders who enacted a love story culminating with a marriage, all in very colourful costume and music again by the locals on wooden instruments and drums. The whole thing was of a very interesting and high standard.

After the performance in the open air, we were invaded by the locals, selling colourful blouses or shirts, very cheap. I spotted one which I liked and asked how much, and was impressed by the price and immediately bought one of the same intricate design (we were told later that you were expected to bargain with them and knock the price down), but I was well satisfied, more so when we arrived back on board Marco Polo, where I found my purchase included matching trunks. I have used them in the garden when it has been a suitably hot day, and brings back happy memories of Bali and Semarang.

<u>6th Day</u>. January 10th. We moved on to Borobudur Temple which was completely swallowed up, covered up and was lost by jungle growth, but was rediscovered, cleared of jungle growth by Raffles, who went on to organise and rebuild it to its former glory. It is now a massive building or arrangement of huge stones and very large and impressive.

Most of the surrounding countryside is dense jungle, some rice fields, some exotic fruits, Longans, each fruit protected by a plaited rush basket, to protect them from the birds, perhaps 200 baskets to a tree. The locals are obviously very active horticulturalists. Lots of these fruits could be purchased from shops and stalls at the road side. Along the road side, there were also some large and hefty-looking trees which Roy told us were mahogany trees. All these strange trees we saw were promptly recognised and named as we proceeded, giving a running commentary, which made the holiday all the more interesting.

<u>7th and 8th Days</u>. January 11th and 12th. Bali. A long journey through dense jungle, rice fields, these being very carefully and efficiently looked after. Also, we passed a number of active volcanoes. We stopped at a wayside establishment similar to our coffee houses, where we were given drinks and looked at the various tourist trinkets and articles for sale.

After this, we were back on the bus and carried on until we arrived at our destination for a midday meal, a large restaurant overlooking a jungle-matted ravine on the other side of which was an active volcano, smoking away from small holes in the sides. In 1994, this volcano erupted, killing about 60 of the local community. We had a very good meal, different, but as always, very enjoyable. After this, we returned to the boat and lifted anchor and were on our way once again.

9th Day. January 13th. We landed on Komodo. This is a very interesting island, inasmuch as it is inhabited by Dragons, real live dragons, fearsome-looking creatures and equally dangerous; we were lucky to visit this island as we were told that our visit was to be the last visit by holiday-makers as it was upsetting the life of these unique animals. They were unknown to the outside world until 1927, when a First World War pilot was flying over these islands and made a forced landing on Komodo. He was obviously very fortunate to get down and survive the landing, as the whole island is covered with dense jungle. However, friends and relatives missed him and knowing his intentions and route, organised searches, but were unsuccessful and so he spent 7 or 8 months on the island, but some of his relatives persisted in their search and eventually found him and took him back to civilisation. But when he started talking about real live dragons, they thought his 7 months of isolation plus his appearance when they found him, had driven him nuts. But eventually, after he had been cleaned and restored to good health and still persisted with his story, he was eventually given serious credibility and an investigation was organised and found to be true. They found these animals up to 12 ft in length, short legs about 2 ft long with a head and mouth like a mincing machine, can eat a whole deer, bones, antlers, the lot in 15 minutes; they can also swim and have managed to swim across to the adjoining island, and now known as the Komodo dragons. The other story that is told to visitors is of a doctor who, like us, visited the island and wandered off the path in the jungle, and all they found of him was his hat and camera.

We were led through the jungle, which was a treat for me because we saw a lot of epiphytic orchids, mostly Vandas, growing on the trees, beautiful. I had two cameras, one for colour slides, a new camera, and one for black-and-white, so I carefully took pictures of these as we progressed. After about 2 miles walking through the jungle, we came to an enclosure which we entered, and about 50 yards away they had placed some sort of raw meat, which the dragons were eating. Once we were all safely in the enclosure, they brought two tins full of water close to the enclosure and then after they had eaten all the meat, they came over to drink. All the visitors now were busy taking photographs. The only problem was neither of the films had gone through my cameras. This was largely due to the fact that they were new cameras and I was not used to them, but it was very disappointing, probably the jewel in the crown of the holiday, and no photographs. But they are certainly fearsome beasts with razor-like teeth and claws to match. One of our party had a heart attack in the compound, and had to be carried by stretcher back to the boat.

<u>10th Day</u>. January 14th. We landed on another island, Larantuka, Flores. We went to the lift on our deck, which took us down to a lower deck near the water line; we were assisted through a door in the side of our ship on to one of the motorised lifeboats, which had been lowered to the water. This part of our trip ashore was very interesting as nobody was involved, but all was completed by one of the ship's officers with a handset, operating the davits and lowering the boat, all very impressive.

Larantuka is very primitive. A small town, rough, unmade roads. It had a church which we visited and in there, we were approached by three young people, who we gathered were students who knew some English. They seemed keen to speak to us, and insisted on exchanging addresses, asking us to write to them. They were about 16-17 years of age. After this, we looked through the town and shops, but as I have said very primitive, and we then went back to the Marco Polo and the luxuries of the modern world.

In the evenings, dinner was an impressive occasion, everyone in their evening dress, a very good orchestra, and waiters all from that part of the world, some of them also taking part in the entertainment.

On days when we cruised through the islands, there were various entertainments available. I found the bar pretty good as there was a very good pianist, playing mostly light classics, but I had some difficulty as a diabetic, I can only drink soft sugar-free drinks or ½ pint of beer or a single whisky.

In the mornings, all our group had the use of a room to meet, when one of our three horticultural specialists, but always headed by Roy Lancaster or Matthew Biggs, operated a question time. Some people produced plants or pieces of a tree they had acquired on their visits to the various islands. Always very interesting. This was always held in the Raffles Lounge.

<u>11th Day</u>. January 15th. Crossed the Equator and passed through the numerous islands in the Flores Sea. We were also invited to the Bridge to see the automatic controls of the Marco Polo. All very impressive like the rest of the boat – all automatic, with a screen which at all times showed any solid object, rock or land under, in front, and each side of the boat, especially at this time, among these islands. But this boat never stops, cruising round the world constantly picking up new groups of holiday-makers and one of the cruises goes down to the Antarctic where, I suppose, with the ice floes, all these sophisticated controls come into good use.

After this, we left the islands and made our way over to Australia via the Timor Sea and on January 16th, we landed at Darwin.

<u>13th Day</u>. January 17th. Tour of Darwin and Botanic Gardens. Here again, with the presence of Roy Lancaster, we were

expected and received with warmth, followed with a conducted tour of the gardens. Wonderful collections of plants and trees. We also visited Kakadu National Park, seeing lots of wallabies and termite hills. We were warned not to disturb or frighten the wallabies as they are known to die of fright or heart attack if disturbed. After this we re-embarked on the bus and continued on our way, passing lots of huge termite hills.

We stopped for lunch at a small community and group of shops and café, where we were fed and refreshed. After lunch we walked for a short time, and at the end of the shops was a man with a huge, massive Water Buffalo Bull, which he told us was the animal used in the film Crocodile Dundee. It was a very impressive animal with horns approximately 10 ft from tip to tip. He then asked if any of our group would like to sit on its back and have a photo taken, but there were no takers and then my daughter, Margaret volunteered, and I took some photos, which I still have for proof.

<u>14th Day</u>. January 18th. Cruised the Arafura Sea.

<u>15th Day</u>. January 19th. Landed on Thursday Island, where we met a young woman who came from Thrapston with a brother in Kettering and she had also lived on the same road in London, when Margaret lived and worked there.

<u>16th Day</u>. January 20th. We landed and boarded a smaller ferry boat which took us out to a floating platform on the Barrier Reef, where we were again transferred to glass-bottomed boats to see corals and fish. There was a section of water enclosed by safety nets and anyone who wished, could go snorkelling with suitable equipment supplied. Here Margaret tried it and took some interesting photographs.

<u>17th Day</u>. January 21st. Cruised to Cairns. The Marco Polo is a 22,000 ton cruise liner and has a heated outdoor swimming pool. We left the Marco Polo here and it carried on from here to New Zealand. We had a full day tour of Kuranda and a scenic

railway trip. This was a very interesting old railway track built to accommodate the Gold Rush times in the 1800s, all very interesting. We had a trip up the river, saw and heard kookaburras and some crocodiles basking on rocks in the sun.

18th Day. January 22nd. Flew from Cairns to Sydney. Everywhere we went in the hotels and on the boat, all the tables in the dining rooms and bathrooms, etc. everywhere there were vases of the Vanda Orchid and pink and white beautifully-marked flowers – Miss Jhokins hybrid. I do not know who she was or is, but if she is anything like the flowers, she must be a smasher. Outside there were lots of Bougainvillaeas all colours, Hibiscus, Sitostakis – Lip-Stick Palm, Delonix – Flame Tree, flowers everywhere.

19th Day. January 23rd. We had a trip round Sydney Harbour, a large area of water, with a narrow entrance from the sea. All the wealthy Australians have large houses and gardens round the beaches with the huge monumental bridge and Opera House in the background, a truly beautiful place.

In the afternoon we had a conducted tour of Sydney Botanical Gardens. More beautiful flowers. Margaret rang a friend at the far end of the harbour, and arranged to meet her for an evening meal. We caught one of the many water taxis and had an enjoyable evening at one of the many restaurants on the harbour side. The lights on the bridge, the boats, the Opera House, etc. are very spectacular at night. There was a large selection of craft, catamarans, some quite large, some very fast, operating within the harbour limits.

20th Day. January 24th. We were taken on the Blue Mountains Tour on an old Gold Rush railway passing through an area which 18 months previously had been completely destroyed by forest fire, but now had grown again, leaving little or no evidence of the destruction, also they pointed out a ravine, where recently the Forestry Commission had discovered a prehistoric tree growing. Eventually, we arrived at the Blue Mountains Botanic Gardens, interesting, but by now we had seen so many magnificent gardens that these, while being interesting, were not so exciting as some we had already visited. We had our lunch here and then back to the rail terminus and our return journey.

21st Day. January 25th. Today we parted from the main tour, which went on to Ayers Rock, which was described to us as beautiful in the sunset and pleasant to climb the following day. Well, to me, the climbing bit did not appeal, so we decided on the three-day extension to Bangkok.

We flew to Bangkok, and here we had to adjust our watches again. Bangkok is a very busy city, the police in the centre wear gas masks permanently; 10 lanes of traffic, hundreds of three-wheeler taxis, put-puts, all with motors, where previously a man was between the shafts, but no priority, these little vehicles quite happily cutting across all ten lanes of traffic. At this time, huge concrete pillars were being erected across the city and on making enquiries, I was told they were to carry a new overhead road to relieve the traffic congestion. What a good idea, so long as they do something about the atmospheric pollution, but all very interesting – all the very best to the very worst.

Snake farms where you can buy snake's blood as an aphrodisiac. The river was much the same, about ½ mile wide, fast-running, all sorts of rubbish floating down, all sorts of interesting craft, water taxis.

Our hotel was the Royal Orchid Sheraton Hotel, about the largest and best hotel in Bangkok, with a helicopter pad on the roof. An orchid on the pillow every night, food excellent. The week after we returned home, to my surprise, there was the reception area of Bangkok Sheraton on the television screen. The man who had got himself into difficulties at Barings Bank had found himself a temporary bolt hole at our hotel.

22nd Day. January 26th. We had a coach trip through Bangkok and out to the floating market. We transferred to a water taxi and took a tour of the canals and floating markets, very interesting, like a giant Venice: canals off the main river, with all sorts of houses and residential properties on stilts, some housing, some obviously well-off owners, down to some who are not so well-off, with the wooden foundations going rotten and sinking into the swamp. We visited a coconut processing area, producing coconut oil and various by-products, very primitive. They say that every bit of a coconut is used, nothing wasted. Close by was an orchid farm, where I purchased some Vandas.

23rd Day. January 27th. We had a river taxi trip to a nice barge where we had a meal, largely of fresh fruit.

24th Day. January 28th. Margaret and I hired another river taxi, and found another orchid farm, and bought some more orchids. The water taxis are a wonderful experience, like large gondolas, with a huge motor somehow balanced on the back end of the craft, which seats about 20 people. A shaft about 10 ft long projects from the motor with a propeller on the end. The driver revs the engine, lifts the engine, which dips the propeller into the water, and off you go at something like 40 miles per hour. When passing another boat, the propeller is lifted from the water by lowering the motor and so on. It is rather exciting and the drivers are very proficient. The front of the taxi lifts high out of the water, and a huge wave each side of the bows is formed, when travelling at speed. Occasionally, the odd splash of water comes into the boat and if it lands on your face, it tends to make you spit as the water looks more like sewage.

I think this city, with all its different avenues of interest, was probably, the most interesting place we visited. Our hotel, all the very latest, to the worst of squalor in other parts of the city and its waterways.

Fred Blount
January 2003
Fred Blount Memoirs 20

www.ingramcontent.com/pod-product-compliance
Lightning Source LLC
Chambersburg PA
CBHW030327080526
44584CB00012B/742